CW00508053

STRONG IN THE SKIN I'M IN

My Vitiligo Skin Journey

STRONG IN
THE SKIN
I'M IN
My Vitiligo Skin Journey

By Joti Gata-Aura

The right of Joti Gata-Aura to be identified as author of this work has been asserted by the author in accordance with the Copyright, Designs and Patents Act 1988

Copyright © 2021 Joti Gata-Aura

All rights reserved. No part of this publication may be reproduced, distributed, or transmitted in any form or by any means, including photocopying, recording, or other electronic or mechanical methods, without the prior written permission of the publisher, except in the case of brief quotations embodied in critical reviews and certain other noncommercial uses permitted by copyright law. For permission requests, write to the publisher at the address below.

Published by Just Jhoom! Ltd
PO Box 142
Cranleigh, Surrey
GU6 8ZX
www.justjhoom.co.uk

Cover Design: Angela Basker
Cover Photograph: Alison J Burrows
Author Photo: Lightning Media
Positively Diverse Branding: Rachel Kepinska-Smith

ISBN: 9798532847767

Dedication

To my beautiful children Ria and Dilan.
May you grow up with confidence and courage in all that
you aspire to do and have love for yourselves as you grow
up in a forever-challenging world that lays ahead of you.
To my beautiful husband, thank you for always
sticking by my side and to my supportive family,
thank you for always believing in me.

Table of Contents

Foreword

What label have you attached to yourself lately?

We live in a world dominated by labels assigned to us throughout our lives, and they reflect and influence how others perceive our identities and how we perceive ourselves. Many of the labels we use to define each other are based on unfounded assumptions and stereotypes. We constantly assign labels to people we hardly know or have never met, and we are subjected to the same treatment. For better or worse, labels signify an effect on our identity over which we have little control.

Labels aren't always bad; they can sometimes represent desirable traits, provide useful expectations, and help us achieve meaningful goals in our lives. As an inclusion practitioner specialising in disability inclusion, I have had the pleasure of working with the most compassionate, self-aware and authentic people. People who believe in humanity over labels and are striving everyday to make the world that we live in a fairer more equitable place.

My intersectional activism is inspired by the barriers I have and continue to face as a South Asian woman who experiences disability. I have taken change into my own hands and founded numerous organisations to improve representation and challenge social inequality globally:

1. Diversability, an inclusive platform providing discounts for disabled people, reducing the financial pressures from the unavoidable extra costs of living with a condition or impairment.

2. Asian Woman Festival, smashing stereotypes and stigma to empower and celebrate South Asian women and underrepresented genders.

3. Asian Disability Network, a support platform around disability, exploring how we navigate this with our ethnic and cultural identity.

I met Joti, who attended a supper club I had organised for Asian Woman Festival. As soon as Joti started to share her story, it instantly resonated with me. Despite our lives and experiences being vastly different, the exclusion and judgement we had faced were due to the same reason. We looked different. I have a short stature of 3'10 due to a rare genetic condition I was born with, and Joti developed a skin condition called Vitiligo. Both are obvious conditions due to which we have both been negatively labelled in our lives.

Disability and any physical or intellectual difference face an even further sense of stigma in South Asian communities because historically, in many Asian countries, it has been considered a taboo or shameful thing. Sadly, these attitudes have mainly remained unchallenged and have been passed down through generations meaning progress on disability inclusion has been painstakingly slow and overdue.

This is primarily due to a lack of education and understanding of the issue itself. Another significant barrier to progress is having terminology for disability, impairments and conditions in South Asian languages because they simply don't exist. Instead, I have repeatedly heard very derogatory and humiliating terminology to describe a condition or impairment.

Religious beliefs and cultural practices are among the most defining elements of belonging and identity in South Asian communities. For example, some people believe disability is a punishment from God or a test to be endured for eternal reward.

So, when I meet people like Joti who have faced similar experiences to me and are helping to challenge perceptions and change the narrative, it gives me an enormous feeling of solidarity. When Joti told me, she had written a book, I was so excited because I know how powerful Joti's story is and how passionate she is in championing issues she cares about such as body positivity, vitiligo awareness and representation.

As you read this book, you will see that courage has been the guiding quality in Joti's journey. Joti has opened up her entire life and the lessons learnt in a sincere, honest and humble way. There is something for everyone to take away from this book, and I hope you find this book as heartening and enlivening as I did.

With much love
Shani Dhanda

Introduction

I never saw a solution, nor did I foresee that life would ever change. This white spot was going to take over my life, and I had no control over what was happening to me. I was always such a positive person, but Vitiligo stole this freedom away from me.

In this book, I share the experience of how, aged 20, my life took a drastic turn for the worse. I talk about this wretched skin condition, which I resented for years but then grew to love, and my subsequent transition into a completely different person. Perhaps now I may even be perceived as overly-confident.

I share the highs and lows of my life: what it is like to hide from the world and yet still strive high, how I managed to achieve all the things I wanted to in life, and how I share my knowledge and give support to those who need it the most. I share my strength, courage and love with those who are struggling because they look different.

By exploring my personal journey to success, in spite of a condition that stripped me of my identity, confidence and courage, I offer light and guidance to all.

Some names have been changed to protect the identities of some people. At no time whilst writing this book did I want to hurt anyone or cause any distress. If I have inadvertently done so, then I give my sincere apologies.

I believe that a story should be told from a place of truth. This story is my truth.

Joti Gata-Aura
London, 2021

Chapter 1 – The White Spot

"The truth is, you don't know what is going to happen tomorrow. Life is a crazy ride and nothing is guaranteed."
Eminem[1]

There is a white spot at the top of my left arm. Why have I not seen this before?

I had never seen anything like it.

It does look a little strange, how odd that it has just appeared out of the blue.

My spot was pale, round and bright — probably about the size of a one pence piece. Little did I know that this would change everything: the central point to myriad anxious conversations with so many people in later life.

I was in Spain, on the balcony, with my best friend Sara*. We had already spent part of the evening examining the white spot on my arm, but I was more concerned that this could just be the tip of the iceberg. *How many more were there?* Nervously, I headed to the bathroom, stripped down to my underwear, and started to inspect my body.

*Name has been changed to protect identity

My head was twisting and turning, like a chicken pecking at its feathers, as I carefully examined the spot. After thoroughly checking myself over, this white, shiny, mark sat visibly under the tan on my left arm like it had been there all my life. Conspicuous, but fortunately alone.

I made my way back to the apartment balcony where Sara was waiting, concerned. Her head moved closer as she stared at the miniature discoloration. Then my questions began.

"Sara, what is this? Look at it!" I said jabbing the top of my arm.

Sara looked at me, perplexed, with questions of her own. "Did you just notice it now? Are you sure it hasn't been there for longer?"

Sara was clearly concerned. Even though she didn't do it there and then, I am sure that she went to check her own body later too. Did she also have this white spot? Maybe we had both eaten the same food, which had caused the spot to appear, and hers was simply in a place she was unaware of.

We must have spent about three hours or so just talking about the spot. It was just something that seemed to bring itself in and out of our conversation, but despite some preoccupation and curiosity, I did not feel overly worried about it at this stage.

Later, this too just passed me by. We continued with our evening, on the balcony of our modest, but centrally-located apartment in Granada, sipping red wine as the sun set beneath our eyes. As thoughts of the spot faded, we giggled as we reminisced about the exhilarating last ten months spent in Spain.

The town center had a real Spanish smell. I had become accustomed to the exotic aromas of fruit, which would drift in through the windows of our flat and harmonize beautifully with our local *bocata*. On the evening in question, we had just finished eating what tended to be our usual Sunday snack (it's a sort of bread roll sandwich), which we would sometimes order, rather than make, when we were feeling particularly lazy.

It was nothing fancy, but the bread was fresh, warm, and crispy. Better still, the bread roll takeaway made the kind of tortilla rolls that could turn a good weekend into a great one. It was probably on the healthier end of the scale as far as fast-food takeout went, or at least this is what we told ourselves: both of us deep down knew that this was an excuse and that we were packing ourselves with calories. Not that we minded.

I remember the chats that Sara and I had on the subject, repeating the mantras that remain engraved in my head to this day.

"Joti, we are going to end up back in London big and round."

Even though we ate healthily during the week, we had a tendency to overindulge in our weekend culinary adventures: *bocata* was very much a part of that routine.

As we spoiled ourselves with this Sunday treat, we often talked about the wonderful times spent during the year. Young as we were, the experience had changed us both as people, allowing us to grow up, find ourselves and discover who we really were. It was the first experience for either of us living abroad: we discussed the realities of being away from our families and how this had strengthened us and turned us into confident young women, perfectly prepared for the challenging world that lay ahead of us.

For me at least, the twelve months spent in Granada was not just an extended trip abroad, it was the authentic adventure that I had always dreamt of. Finally, I had made this dream come true.

While on our year abroad, Sara and I both studied Spanish at Granada's university. Although we had the option to work, we both chose to study during our time in Spain, which gave us some flexibility. Although most of our week was spent at the university, we would always research and plan our exhilarating weekend breaks, looking forward with ever more excitement to our next weekend adventure.

We wanted to make the most of our year in Spain and had plans to visit several of the 17 different autonomous regions in the country. I have always been fascinated by the cultural differences not just between the people in different regions, but between those who live in the major cities — like Barcelona, Madrid, and Malaga — and those who live rurally. I was very keen to ensure I would really get to explore these cultural differences and really make the most of the opportunities my year abroad brought me.

I was always grateful to have parents who fully supported my education and my decision to study languages in particular. Many of their generation and culture would not have deemed this a route to a proper career. I knew that I was not conforming to the South

Asian "expectations" of becoming a doctor or lawyer, and while these were routes that many of my friends and family chose to take (and whilst I fully respected their decision), I realise I was lucky to have parents who encouraged my passion and drive for a career in languages. I knew I was going to make something of my life with languages at the centre, so this was my goal right from the start.

My love of languages and passion for travel went hand-in-hand. During the year, Sara and I would organize cheap bus tours that would take us to different cities, where we would explore the sites and gain a real understanding of the Spanish culture.

"Where shall we go next?" Sara would always ask, eagerly suggesting places she thought I would like.

For one of our trips, we ventured to Madrid, a journey from Granada that took us some five hours. I will always remember the excitement. Even though we had embarked on such a long journey, the adrenaline would not let us sleep at all on the weekends.

Our long coach journeys would be filled with chat and laughter as we sat comfortably on the cosy coach that took us to our destination through breath-taking views of the country.

It's strange to think I enjoyed it so much, because, oddly enough, I have never been someone who enjoys taking coaches. The couple of times I needed to use coaches in London, I would feel sick and claustrophobic, but I was always impressed with the coach services in Spain. The tickets were always priced fairly, and you would be provided with good quality seats and air conditioning inside which made longer trips manageable. You could also fully recline the seats and there always appeared to be more space given for passengers than I was used to.

Sometimes we would simply natter away, other times we observed the beautiful landscapes of Spain: endless mountainous regions of arid land and a surprising amount of agriculture. These trips allowed me to understand the abundance of food that is grown there, much of which is then exported to the UK — how lucky the Spanish are to grow and cultivate most of their own fresh organic produce!

Everything I saw enriched my experience and made me fall in love with the country even more. I gained an appreciation for nature and our interaction with it: the surroundings of the countryside were immensely peaceful, and I grew exceptionally fond of them.

Our trips cross-country taught us about the differences between the north and south of Spain. Similar to the UK, the contrast is striking: the Northerners are more reserved, less chatty, and seemingly reticent to communicate or get to know you, but the Southerners were a whole different ball game. The more I grew to understand the cultural divide, the more of a connection I felt with people in the south. Their amiability drew me, and eventually I wanted to visit more cities there than in the north.

"Why don't we go to Sevilla?" asked Sara. She explained that the coach journey wouldn't be too arduous from Granada and was enthused about the city's abundant culture and history. I did not even think twice. Within four days, we had our tickets booked and bags packed — ready to explore this incredible city and eagerly waiting for the week to end.

After a long, but comfortable coach trip, Sara and I arrived on a hot spring morning in Sevilla. Bright, bold colors adorned the houses of the town centre, with tourists swarming everywhere. The town is a popular destination even for Spanish tourists, and I could see why: I immediately fell in love with the place and the warmth of its people. We were overwhelmed by the breathtaking sights we encountered, above all the courtyards full of orange trees, which we learned was typical in Andalucia.

We planned to pack all our sightseeing into one main day: our trip started with *La Giralda*, one of the city's iconic and primary viewpoints. Then it was swiftly onto the *Real Alcázar*, located in the heart of Sevilla. This would reveal a lavish-looking palace, one of the oldest still in use in the world. We were enthralled.

"I've never seen anything like this, Sara," I gasped, as we carefully and quietly walked inside the palace's exquisite rooms decorated with tiling and impressive ceilings and looked over its remarkable gardens.

"I knew you would love Sevilla," Sara beamed as she gaped at the ceilings of the palace. As we made our way through the different rooms of the palace, Sara whispered in my ear that it was time to move on: we still needed to get to the *Plaza de España* and the rest of the sights on our plan. I knew I wanted to get the most of our sightseeing done in the day, as we would be out in the evening. And, in case things got late and we did not wake up early the next morning, at least we would have seen the main sights.

The *Plaza de España* is a very famous square in the Maria Luisa Park and, naturally I suppose, a real tourist attraction. Shaped in a semicircle, it's probably the most impressive landmark of the city after the cathedral. It's huge, too: the size of 5 football pitches. So, during our visit we really had to plan in enough time to see all of it.

I had never seen anything like it: such a vast place, with a magnificent central balcony — brick-built with Moorish features that made it stand out. I loved everything about the *Plaza de España:* a great place to escape the city's hustle and bustle. The locals love it too.

The day's tour concluded, and thoughts turned to the evening, deciding where to dine and where to put on our party shoes. Nightlife was important to our cultural visits, as was the planning of popular places to visit in the evenings.

We were just 20, so our party life was something we really looked forward to. Our evenings would be full of conversations and laughter: in beautiful, authentic *tapas* bars, surrounded by people talking loudly and excitedly. This is quite common in Spain, but we loved to be amongst people who appeared to be arguing passionately about a certain topic or simply talking at a very loud volume. It became the norm wherever we went: I learned that this was just what Spanish people were like and gradually transformed into someone who communicated with passion (and at a slightly louder volume than normal) myself. Perhaps this is why some of my friends call me loud nowadays: I feel this is a personality trait that became a part of me while living in Spain!

Our *tapas* evenings brought the whole experience to life and we would relish the food presented to us when eating out. *Las empanadas* were my favorite: delicious *tapas* that were regularly served whenever one purchased a drink. They consisted of a mixture of chicken or vegetables, deep-fried with cheese, but I would later learn that *tapas* would vary from region to region — in Sevilla I made sure I tried the mouth-watering Iberian ham. It was great just to pay for a drink and have all these little snacks on the side to accompany it.

It was something I thought restaurants at home could definitely learn from. *Where in the UK would you ever get free food?* I wondered. I relished the experience and ensured that we regularly went out for *tapas* whenever we were able to, especially on the weekend trips.

Afterwards, we were invariably out and dancing to some authentic Spanish music. I was starting to embrace Spanish dance music and even found myself buying some music collections by Alejandro Sanz, an artist who was very popular at that time and sang a lot of love songs. It was great for language learning too. I loved exploring the new words in the songs, learning what they meant, then singing along to the song in Spanish. It was a real accomplishment to learn the words off by heart, then go out and sing along fluently.

During our time together in Granada, my friendship with Sara developed very quickly, becoming more like a relationship between sisters in the end. I depended on Sara and I often needed her emotional support: although the Spanish were welcoming, this was not my country and I did feel homesick at times.

Our weekend in Sevilla went by in the blink of an eye. The city certainly left its mark, a truly special place even among the other wonderful settlements we had visited. Our trips did not end there though. From Sevilla we visited the magical island of Ibiza, the third largest of Spain's Balearic Islands in the Western Mediterranean. I had longed to visit this island since I was 16, influenced by documentaries on how the British would venture to Ibiza solely for the nightlife. It looked incredible and I wanted to experience the exact same. We really loved dance music, and Ibiza had everything you could dream of, even on a tiny island.

It wasn't just the clubs, the nature was breathtaking, and the cuisine and culture were fantastic as well. There seemed to be something on offer for everyone; people traveling on relaxing retreats and those longing to experience the nightlife. The place was so very enchanting, and I wanted to stay for longer, but we had university to get back to.

The more Sara and I spent time and traveled with each other and the closer we grew, the more afraid I became of leaving and going back to the "real world". After a while, it was continuously on my mind. Having lived through all these incredible experiences together, how was life going to be from now on?

One evening on the balcony, we looked despondently at each other, talking about just how quickly the year had passed and expressing sadness at the realisation that we would be moving back to the UK very soon. There, we would be with our families again and would not have each other by our sides any longer. It was a strange feeling. I leaned on Sara for support, and she was someone who was always there for me.

So how did I end up with Sara abroad? Well, they say you always connect to people who are like you, and I believe this is what drew me to Sara. She was someone who I had instantly connected with on my first day at

Queen Mary University, London, in the Humanities block.

I will never forget her warm and gentle smile when I first spoke to her, lost, asking whether I was in the humanities block.

"Well, I really hope so. This is where I am supposed to be as well!" she said, laughing.

"Really?" I said gratefully.

I was probably more excited than the situation really warranted, but I felt reassured to have met someone on my course so quickly, especially as the whole block was full of unfamiliar faces. This made me feel a little nervous. I never considered myself to be shy by any means, but seeing all these new people, in a strange modern new building where I would be studying my degree, made me feel slightly insecure and tense. Sara's friendly face instantly put me at ease.

Sara was pretty. She had a figure that most girls probably dreamed of: slim, petite and with well-defined, dark Spanish features. Her piercing brown eyes, prominent cheekbones and beautiful thick, chestnut hair completed the look.

I did feel a little envious at times. Sara was Spanish and studying her own language, which meant that our degree would be much easier for her. After all, she did not have to learn many new words, her fluency was perfect, and she did not have any difficulty in understanding complex grammatical structures. On the other hand, I would spend hours in books, trying hard just to comprehend their meaning. This did make me a tiny bit resentful; I wasn't even entirely sure why she needed a degree in Spanish.

However, I knew that Sara was someone I could reach out to for support, and she was always there for me. This is the foundation to any good friendship, but ultimately what would strengthen our bond even further. We would spend our evenings mingling with other students at the student union or venture into Central London to visit two of the very popular Spanish bars at the time. We were experiencing life as students and enjoying high society.

Bar Madrid was one of our regular Central London bars. It was a quirky, but charming nightclub situated in the heart of London, always packed with people. Sara introduced me to the place: she absolutely loved it there and we both adored dancing to the Spanish music and letting our hair down after a long, tiring week of lectures.

Although I got to know many other students, I always seemed to have much more in common with Sara, perhaps because our cultures connected, and we felt we could understand one another.

One day, Sara asked me whether I would like to go out for her brother's graduation one Friday evening. I invited a few friends along and we decided to go. Eager to please and eager to party, I decided on an outfit, got dressed up and ventured into the night with my close friends to dance the night away.

That was the evening that Sara introduced me to her family and friends, including one boy in particular: Nev.

I can vividly remember the sudden panic as we were introduced. Nev was a friend of Sara's brother: slim and tall, he towered above me but met my gaze with his soft, kind, brown eyes. These gave a glimpse into his gentle character. Nev was softly-spoken and listened carefully as I told him I was studying Spanish with Sara . He seemed interested in what I was saying, as well as intriguing in his own right, and I remember wanting to know more. The night went by extremely quickly from then on, and as my friends called me back to dance, I never really thought anything of it. I later found out from Sara that the boy had taken quite a liking to me, but even though I thought he was quite cute too, we never acted on anything.

Back at university, we were progressing to our second year, the time when students must decide where to spend their year abroad. Although I was studying a degree in Spanish with French, I did not have to spend any time in France, so I set my sights on traveling to Spain. Even though I had been to Spain before, this had always been in the company of a family, either my own or a "guest family" on Spanish exchange trips. This time though, I would be going alone, and I felt a bit uneasy at the thought of being completely by myself in a foreign country.

I was just starting to panic when, to my amazement, Sara came up with the idea that would immediately alleviate all the tension in my body.

"Joti, why don't we spend our year abroad together? Let's fly out and live in Granada!"

I could hear the excitement in her voice as she looked at me eagerly for a response. I was worried that we wouldn't end up speaking enough Spanish if we went together, but Sara reassured me saying that we would make a concerted effort to always speak in the language while we were there.

Although I told her that I needed time to think about it, it did not take me long to make my decision. That evening, I discussed what I planned to do with my family, and they were fully supportive of my decision. As a parent myself now, I know they would have been worried about their daughter flying out alone, but I knew they felt reassured after Sara and I planned for our families to meet. Our idea was that this would eliminate any residual worries about me living in a foreign country alone.

Within a week of making my decision, I was flying out to Spain with Sara. I know she was just as excited as I was.

We lived a spectacular life in the South of Spain. In Granada, the weather would start getting warmer from March onwards and the summers would be scorching hot. I never quite fully appreciated how lucky we were to live in the sunshine; in fact, I would complain to Sara that it was too hot to do anything. I did tan and was two shades darker than my normal tone.

Maybe the white patch had something to do with skin pigmentation from the sun?

There it was again. I wanted to put the patch behind me and not let it ruin the last few days of what had begun to feel like a prolonged holiday. I was due to return to London and starting to feel all sorts of emotions: happiness and excitement were tinged with sadness, as I knew I would be leaving this beautiful country, which I had fallen in love with, behind.

Granada has a whitewashed city center, dashed with flamboyant colors and laced with smells wafting down from the mountainous region that encircled the flat agricultural land. Our flat was centrally located, close to the Alhambra, considered by some to be one of the ten wonders of the world. The city itself was full of gardens and rich architecture, which fascinated me deeply.

Southern Spain offered such a rich culture, and the people there were so welcoming, more so than I ever felt in the north. I was truly lucky to have experienced this life and I embraced every day of it.

Studying Spanish was a dream come true. I had loved languages from a young age, and now I was here, living the Spanish way of life and enjoying the country's culture and customs. I fell in love with this beautiful language when I was 14 years old, after I was given the opportunity to study Spanish at school.

A year after studying Spanish at secondary school, my teacher suggested I apply for a Spanish scholarship at the University of Madrid. I was confused. *Really me?* I wondered, unsure whether I really had the talent to succeed. Within a week I received my offer.

"Mum, Dad you will not believe this!" I exclaimed. I told them all about the scholarship, which was given to just five people in the UK.

My family was proud of me, and this was the first moment I remember feeling a huge sense of achievement. It was exhilarating.

The program itself was exciting too: a month at the University of Madrid, aged just 14. I kept repeating this to myself and could not sleep for weeks as adrenaline raced through my body.

The experience was sensational: I was learning Spanish at the *Complutense de Madrid,* living in the halls of accommodation, and at the epicenter of an eye-opening experience that would give me a true flavor of what was to come later.

After just a year, I embarked on a Spanish exchange trip that would change my vision of language learning forever. That week abroad was the most enriching experience I had ever had: I bonded with my Spanish exchange immediately and just immersed myself into the family's culture for a whole week.

I was placed with a family who could not speak English to any great extent, which was the most perfect opportunity for me to gain a better understanding of the language. I didn't know it at the time, but my Spanish exchange would turn into a lifelong friend who attended my wedding as a bridesmaid 14-years later!

We spent every holiday writing to each other, each of us helping to improve the other's language skills. I loved the feeling of being across countries, waiting for our letters to reach each other's houses. I returned to Spain twice afterwards, with my exchange coming to visit me too. She loved how my family was like hers.

She isn't the only person to have noticed the similarities between Spanish and Indian culture. Through my exchange trip and my other visits to Spain, I also noticed that the cultures were similarly connected. Family plays a big part in this — incredibly important in the Spanish and Indian cultures alike — with older generations instilling their beliefs in education and work ethic in the younger ones.

Success is managed through education, the route to a better life. However, work-life balance matters too: the Spanish place great value on time spent with family, with respect and family pride at the forefront.

Obviously, the Spanish diet is considerably different from Indian cuisine, but it is often a question of how, rather than what. At lunchtime in Spain, families would come home to spend lunch together and enjoy home cooked food by their mothers. This is a custom that has gone on for decades, in addition to the well-known siestas: a custom in some regions of Spain where everything closes between the hours of 12p.m. and 1.30p.m.

The importance of families coming together was and still is key. I found this very similar to the Indian traditions I knew, in that sitting down and eating together is an important part of the day. I still hold these values close to my heart: being with my family at dinner time reminds me about the importance of sharing feelings on how the day has been. This sense of togetherness is incredibly important. It allows for children to be heard and understood, confident that they are being listened to. I experienced this as a child and it is now part of my own family life.

If you need anything during lunchtime hours in Spain, tough luck. Town centres turn into ghost towns, with shutters closed on shops, businesses and schools and people at home. I was very fond of this: families prioritized spending time with each other, eating a home cooked, healthy lunch and making conversation together around the table.

The Spanish seem to place more importance on what other people think about them. This is a "forever issue" in Indian culture, where families judge one another and gossip about health, marriages, and the lives of others. Spanish culture has similarities in this regard, as families talk often about one another. Mostly this is harmless, but it can often turn into negativity and gossiping. Stories are manipulated by one person and changed into another story by another.

For all its peculiarities, I always felt at home in a culture so close to my own. My identity was perhaps an issue — I stood out due to the color of my skin — but I never really encountered real racism whilst I was there.

Sundays were usually a little busier. In the city centre, families were out and about, taking strolls together. I loved this way of life, people just enjoying being together as a family. I was so used to everyone being busy that I thrived on seeing the quality time that families would have.

Visiting and living in Spain contributed to my love of a culture and country that I always longed to return to. I had become accustomed to the siestas, the low cost of living, healthier lunches at three and late-night *tapas* at ten. All in all, I had really enjoyed settling into a new life there.

However, the time was drawing to a close. What would happen when I returned to London? How would I re-adapt to my London life? Was this white spot going to fade and disappear? With this cocktail of emotions, and unsure just what was in store for me, I returned to the UK.

Chapter 2 – Happiness Before the Patch

*"It is the sweet, simple things of life
which are the real ones after all."*
Laura Ingalls Wilder[2]

I was just a regular girl, brought up in a loving family. I grew up more or less without technology, my summers spent at Crystal Palace Park, which my parents would book for me over the summer. These summer holidays would be filled with a whole range of fun-filled activities, including table tennis, badminton, and swimming. Crystal Palace was the perfect place to keep myself entertained, and looking back on the time now, it provided me with some amazing skills while benefiting my health and fitness and keeping my mind active and engaged.

This is the life I envisage for my children too, which is why it worries me that so many children do not have the opportunity to be more engaged in sports and fitness. It's just so crucial for a healthy lifestyle.

We had all that we needed. I was brought up in a humble, down-to-earth way by my supportive and loving family. My parents were extremely hard-working: my mother was a medical professional and thus had great expertise in preparing good, nutritious food.

"Joti make sure you eat the right foods; these will keep you healthy and strong in the long run." That's what she told me, and she certainly helped too, cooking fresh, home-cooked, nutritious dishes. She knew it would strengthen our immune system and encourage us to be adventurous when it came to trying new things. However, despite my mother's influence, I never really considered nutrition to be overly important until later in life.

Mum always had a passion for cooking and still does. Ever since I can remember, she was always thinking about what to cook, often spending hours in the kitchen making delicious food at weekends.

"What shall I cook tonight?" was a daily question: she was always inquisitive, always keen to bring fresh and innovative menus and ideas to our dining table. The *pranthas* were special though. It was always lovely to watch my mum kneading the dough, then rolling it out evenly before putting it on the frying pan to shallow fry. They were a real weekend treat. Alongside these dishes, mum would combine a variety of vegetables to create mouthwatering aromas with her cooking.

I did not really question my mum about diet and the types of food she cooked at the time. After all, she was very knowledgeable about what foods were good to eat and what part of the body they were good for. I remember that carrots were supposed to be good for the eyes, but different food was served to benefit other parts of my body too.

Some of it has rubbed off. To this day, I keep a concise health chart on my fridge with information about which foods benefit which body parts, educating my children with the same knowledge.

I'm grateful that my mum always cooked food that would benefit my immune system. At the time, I hadn't really looked at the subject closely or considered modifying my diet to stimulate my melanin. This was never really something that was shared in the nascent days of the internet either.

Perhaps today things would be different.

As well as being an experienced cook, mum fielded plenty of phone calls from friends and family, all asking for advice on diet and nutrition. Even today, she is forever on the phone advising people and supporting them with their health and wellbeing. People put their trust in mum, they trust her opinions and she generously takes time from her busy schedule to offer solutions to various ailments and health problems.

One *auntyji* would ask about high blood pressure, the next about osteoporosis and the *auntyji* after that about mental health issues. Mum's list went on and on: it is something I have become accustomed to over time.

Mum was fond of one saying in particular: *you are never too old to learn.* This is a mantra she has lived by: not only was she a qualified medical professional and kept multiple folders of certificates for her medical qualifications, she also embarked on courses ranging from cookery, baking, knitting and reflexology. Being so knowledgeable made mum a great resource when it came to asking for help and support and even now, she is always looking at new skills to learn.

Growing up, I felt proud to have a mum that people turned to. I felt sure she'd be able to offer some advice about my white spot, and I felt disheartened when she told me there was nothing she could do. No healing to offer, no advice to stop the pale patches spreading at such a rapid rate. I wished she could heal me, take my pain away like she did for so many others.

Cooking was something I realise I took for granted, especially now that I am a mum myself. Mum never cooked oven food, it was all handmade from scratch, and she still cooks a range of fusion-style dishes, presented on the table in a rainbow of colour, whenever I'm over. The table heaves with a range of aromas and authentic flavours. I feel I appreciate it more now, particularly because I focus heavily on what I eat and how it is cooked. Food remains a huge part of my life. Something passed on from my mother, through me, to my children.

Funnily enough, Punjabi cooking used to be known for being unhealthy because the food was cooked in deep fat. Although generally speaking this is true, Mum never used to cook like this at home. As early as the early 80's, while most people were still cooking Indian food swimming in oil, Mum had already moved onto a healthier lifestyle. She used less oil in her *sabjis*, Indian vegetable dishes, as well as her *rotis* (also known as chapati), a round flatbread.

Sometimes she baked food, and often she used alternative products to fry certain foods. Although at the time it was uncommon, my dad was hands-on in the kitchen too. He was an expert at cooking meat dishes, and I loved how passionate he was about what he cooked.

Food united my family, brought us together, gave us time to talk at mealtimes. Looking back, these are the days I miss the most.

Everything passes. By the time I reached my mid 20s I was a young woman just like any other, one who loved to dress up and cared about how I looked. I worked part-time during my first year at university, making my way up to Sunday manager at Accessorize. At the time, this was a credible job to have and I felt quite proud of myself.

At Accessorize, I thought I had money management all worked out, but the reality was that I spent over half my wages on clothes and shoes. Looking back, I understand how big a part dressing up played in developing my self-confidence. I loved working in the shop, which was something of a dream job for me aged 21, especially to be so satisfied and proud at progressing to a management role at a young age. I left the position for my year abroad in Spain but returned for my final year in 2001.

I loved going to work, I loved meeting people, but the white patches were spreading, which raised a number of questions: *How was I going to hide these patches from everyone? What would people think?*

I certainly did not feel I could reveal them to anyone. I had to find a way to keep my secret hidden, but how could I possibly manage this with the patches spreading?

Chapter 3 – Failure and Facing Facts

"Failure is the key to success;
each mistake teaches us something."
Morihei Ueshiba[3]

Back in Spain, Sara looked at me gloomily.

"This is it, Joti."

Sara's voice was soft, but I could sense her deflation. Then, suddenly, I broke down into tears. I had been packing my suitcases for over a week, lost in sorrow as I organized my belongings and sorted out which items I would be bringing back to London. I had accumulated a lot of Spanish souvenirs from all the cities I visited. Keyrings were my personal keepsakes, tangible mementos of all the wonderful places we had visited. As I packed them away, I realised I did not want to leave our Bohorquez flat, and I could tell Sara felt the same.

"I can't believe this is it. Our adventure is over."

The sadness drained through me, rather than skating over my skin. It travelled through every cell to reach the ground. An outsider may have thought that this was some sort of relationship breakup and, in honesty, it almost felt like one. Our friendship was stronger than ever. We had lived, studied, eaten, talked, partied, and travelled together. This was a meaningful, honest and genuine bond, and I was going to truly miss Sara.

I also was not quite sure how I was going to readjust back in London. Perhaps it would have been easier with Sara, but when she told me she would not be flying back with me to London, I was devastated. Instead, Sara left for Malaga to stay with her parents over the summer, and the realization kicked in that I would be flying back to London alone.

I really longed for us to be together and fly back to end our year abroad. Some closure, at least. However, Sara's family came to Granada to take her with her to the south. I remember the day I left my apartment in Granada, shutting the brown heavy door behind me and grabbing a taxi drenched in my own melancholy.

However, it wasn't just my suitcase. I would be returning to London with my white patch, which dominated my thoughts as I drifted away on the flight home.

My plane landed back in London Gatwick on June 10, 1999. My eyes filled with tears, but I was so excited to see my parents at the airport. As soon as I reached the arrivals gate, I hugged them so tightly, suddenly realising how much I had missed them.

Sad as I was, a part of me was glad to be back with my home comforts. On the car journey home I reflected on the Martin Bohorquez flat, this exotic, Arabic-style name: difficult to pronounce and taking weeks to get right. I was reminiscing about Spain already, to the extent that I could not quite allow a conversation with my parents to flow. My mind still felt like it was in Spain, even though I was physically in the UK. It would take a while to reconnect back home because I just wanted to relive all the exciting moments.

It passed in a blur. Dad asked about the flight, but I was again preoccupied with my white spot, even if I was not even sure if I would bring it up.

Maybe it will disappear once the tan fades. Surely there's no point in mentioning anything just yet?

I just wanted to close my eyes and return to Spain in my dreams. Perhaps if I never woke up, I could keep my memories alive. However, Spain was about to come back into view: opening the post that had been left in my bedroom, I found one particular letter addressed from the university. I had been expecting some results anyway, so I opened the letter eagerly before staring at the wording in disbelief.

I immediately broke down in tears, scarcely believing what I was reading: according to the letter I had not passed one of my five exams in Granada and would have no choice than to re-sit it. I was devastated. How could this happen?

I attended all my lectures. I submitted all my assignments. There must be a mistake.

But it was no mistake. The wording was unequivocal, not the result of blurry-eye syndrome. As much as I didn't like it, it was simply the truth: I had not done enough to go through to my finals. It felt enough to crush me, break me, destroy me.

How was I going to break the news to my parents? How would they ever understand what was going on during the last month of my exams? I had to push myself to go downstairs and explain everything: from the white patch to me not passing my third year at university.

It was not as if I hadn't worked during the year, so what could have possibly happened? In any case, it felt as if the patch had something to do with it, but whether it was physiologically affecting me or if the worry was just distracting me, I did not know.

I needed someone to talk to. The first person I thought of turning to was Sara. I quickly dialed her home number (we did not have mobiles at the time) so it was more a shot in the dark that I would catch her at home. I needed her to calm me down. My heart was racing, but the first time I called, the house phone yielded no answer.

Maybe she was eating or sleeping. I knew her so well. I went through her routine to work out why she would not answer the phone. Then it dawned on me: she was with her family after months of being away.

I felt bad imposing my issues on her, but I knew I needed to. Sara had been there when we first saw the spot, and she would understand how I was feeling.

I called for the second time and felt a sudden relief when I heard Sara's voice. I missed her badly already, and just hearing her voice reassured me that I was going to be okay. Sara had a comforting voice. She was always one of these people who thought logically about things, reasoned rationally and acted strategically. In other words, the opposite of me. Panic-stricken, all I knew was that I had two issues: my exams and my spot. However, these felt so huge that they simply merged into a world falling apart right in front of me.

"Did you get your results?" I asked her curiously and nervously. I did not even let her respond properly before I told the news of my results. "What am I going to do?" I screeched, before I broke down in tears once more.

Sara had passed her tests, but when I told her I had to re-do the year, she was really upset. As emotion overcame me, I felt unable to speak, thoughts racing through my head.

How am I going to tell my parents; about this and my white patch? What if they do not understand my skin issue? How am I going to get through this?

Sara reassured me that everything was going to be ok and encouraged me to go downstairs to speak to my parents. This was going to be a huge turning point for me, a turning point for the worse.

The conversation ended. I felt I had nothing more to say to Sara, and as we said goodbye my tears did not stop running. The more I cried, the more I realised that it felt like the end of my life, the end of my world as I knew it. I was 20 years old. How could I take a year out? What would this mean?

I did not want to disappoint my parents, who had such high hopes for me. They came to the UK from Kenya in the mid-60s to study. It was an incredible opportunity for my father to come to London at the time: he studied and lived in the affluent area of Chelsea. However, he worked incredibly hard and took his opportunities to work, achieve and strive high.

Both my parents believed a successful life was built upon the fundamentals of good education. It was central to their values. It was not easy for Asian parents in the 60s and 70s to send their children to the UK to study, which I think is why they felt a debt needed to be repaid.

"Joti, you don't know about hard work. We had it hard when we came to the UK," he would always tell me. This may have been true, but it burdened me with a great deal of pressure and a fear of disappointing them. With this news, I knew I would be letting them down hugely.

After procrastinating for an hour, I decided to make my way downstairs. The smells of mum's cooking brought a feeling of home back. I had missed her cooking during my year abroad. The aromas of the *subji* and *roti* oozed through the house, making me feel like I was already ravishing the food she had prepared. This tempting smell pulled me down the stairs by the nose. I was lucky, as I did not have the strength to take each step down myself.

When I finally made it downstairs, Dad was on the phone to some relatives. He was always the one people turned to for advice or support, I knew, but after some considerable time he was still not off the phone. Why was it always Dad they leaned on for support? Why were they always taking up our family time to discuss their issues?

Ultimately, my father was a pillar not only for my immediate family, but for the extended family too. Everyone looked up to him. From financial advice to emotional support, he was the person people felt they trusted. They got sound advice from him, but it always bothered me because he was my Dad and I just wanted his attention. Especially now. It seemed to take forever.

Do I just leave this and come back tomorrow? How will I sleep over this? How can I possibly go to bed not telling them both?

With this thought, Dad ended the call and looked at me with a broad smile on his face: a look of happiness and great excitement. He told me how nice it was for me to be home, which seemed to make what I had to say even worse.

"I need to tell you both something," I murmured. He looked back, uneasily.

I stuttered. I hesitated. I took a deep breath and tried again.

"Dad, I got a letter from university. It says I did not pass one of the exams."

Dad paused and Mum immediately stopped cooking. I could sense the despair. I continued explaining how a month before I was due to take my final modules, I had discovered a white spot on my body.

"White spot?" Dad asked, anxiously.

I told them the whole story. How, a month before I was due to return to London, in the middle of my final exams, I had discovered the patch. I pointed to my left arm and both my parents came over to investigate. Mum was full of medical advice and knowledge, but even she was not quite sure what the answer was.

The conversation about my exams seemed secondary. As we discussed my skin, I could tell that this was concerning my parents far more. This was not what I was expecting, at which point I realised that this could be far more serious than I had thought.

That evening, after several hours discussing my skin, we decided that it would be best for me to visit the GP. Early next morning, Mum made the appointment.

I ended the evening feeling drained and mentally exhausted. This was not how I wanted things to be at home: I did not want to bring home stress and tension, and I did not want to worry my parents. It felt like it was all my fault. Guilt was building and I felt incredibly anxious already in anticipation of the doctor's office the next day.

The next morning, we headed to our GP. On the bus, Mum had so many questions. She asked what I had eaten, whether I had been sitting in the sun without sunblock and so much more.

"The sun could be the cause of the pigmentation you have," she stated, matter-of-factly.

Mum was a medical professional who had studied her way to the top of her field. She knew what she was talking about. I had often wondered why she did not become a doctor, as she was so very educated and knowledgeable about every type of medicine and different types of ailments.

As the bus approached the surgery, I felt relieved to be a little nearer to some closure, because the questioning was creating huge doubt in my mind. Even the ten minutes waiting felt like hours. Just as it felt like the not knowing would kill me. Eventually we were called in.

"Ms Gata-Aura, room number three please."

I felt a shiver down my spine as I rose out of my seat and, together with Mum, entered the office.

"Take a seat," said Dr Halpin in his calm and reassuring voice, "How can I help you today?"

I just stared at her. Then, I gradually stuttered the words out of my mouth.

Chapter 4 – My Diagnosis

"There's so many things that life is,
and no matter how many breakthroughs, trials will exist
and we're going to get through it. Just be strong."
Mary J. Blige[4]

"I 've found this white spot on the top of my left arm."
I paused to lift up my long-sleeved blouse. "I am not
sure what it is, but I have just returned from Spain and
I noticed it a month before I was due to fly back."

"Can I take a look?" asked the GP, looking concerned:
professional, rather than overly empathetic. She asked
her routine questions, as any doctor would, then
paused as she observed my spot.

"It's Vitiligo."

"Vitiligo?" I whispered. Then louder, "What is
Vitiligo?"

The GP then went on to explain the condition further
and to outline the two options to deal with it – either
to leave it as it was and to camouflage the blemishes or
to undergo PUVA treatment.

I was anxious, as I had no idea what PUVA would involve. I looked to mum for reassurance, hoping she would know more. She must have come across this in her medical career, or maybe she knew someone who had undergone it? I felt a glimmer of hope, thinking there may possibly be some of her colleagues at the hospital who would be able to support.

The doctor continued, "It's a light-based treatment that can take several months to cure Vitiligo. However, even then, there is no guarantee of success. It is also likely that the condition will spread."

I found out that PUVA stands for Psoralen Ultraviolet Therapy. The treatment sounded like a foreign language, but the worst part was the possibility of it spreading. My heart sank. I just wanted to run out of the room, to go back home and have a long cry. I needed time to process this devastating news.

The whole bus journey home, Mum and I talked about the options. I sobbed most of the way, thinking about how drastically this small spot could spread. Mum told me that in the whole of her career, she had hardly seen anyone with Vitiligo and that she was really surprised that it had come into our family. I could see that she was worried, but she tried to be the mum that she was: staying strong for me.

I was feeling increasingly pessimistic, so we changed tact to actions, discussing what the best option for me would be. By the time I got home, I had pretty much decided to take the treatment route. Seeing as the spot was relatively new, I had to do everything in my power to get rid of it before it took over. The treatment was the best chance to do this.

My internal monologue took over: *If I do this properly, maybe the spot will just... disappear.*

My mind was made up. I would take a year out of university, focus on my skin and work on obtaining the marks I had missed out on previously. While I wanted to finish my degree properly and be proud of myself, something I knew I could achieve, I still felt very sad that Sara was going through to her finals without me. I would not be spending any more time with her, and the thought devastated me. After a year so close to her, I was not ready to accept being alone.

But, I had to focus on myself, and I had to focus on getting rid of this spot. Fortunately, my parents were eager to support me, and with their approval, taking a year out now did not seem as disastrous as I thought it would be.

The next day, I shot out of bed to call the GP, who immediately referred me to King's College London Hospital. Within two weeks, I had started an intense course of treatment there. I remember thinking, at that point, that I would be ok. I started the first session in September of 1999, which would prove to be the start of many.

I had to be patient and commit to the PUVA for the best chance of success. My family were fully supportive of the decision I had made, but this did not prevent the continuous conversations we would have at home, especially about how my Vitiligo had started. One theory was that this had to be related to the sun. After all, I did not have this patch before I left for Spain, so surely the hot weather was a prime suspect.

I exhaustively researched PUVA before starting the treatment. Long-term, my sessions could lead to side effects as serious as cancer, but I was prepared to take the risk: as far as I saw it, there was no other option available. I always had hope, however small, that it could work for me.

That evening, I decided to get myself online and see what else I could find out about Vitiligo. I took myself up to my parents' room and started to slowly dial up for internet connection. I still vividly remember spending about 10 minutes before being able to connect to the server. This was how the internet was back in 1999, so I never even thought about how long it would take: this was perfectly normal. As I sat there, waiting for connection, I wondered what sort of information would be available for me.

I'd never really thought about going online previously. At that time, technology was not as frequently used as it is today, so it was less of a standard response. As the dial tone signaled that the internet had finally been connected, I typed the word *Vitiligo* into Google. Two pages popped up, enough for me to assure myself that the condition existed even if the information was limited. There was only brief information on the patches and PUVA.

I learned at that time that Vitiligo was an autoimmune condition that affected 1% of the world's population. It could skip a generation, but it was hereditary. I was shocked to discover that other people in the family could have it too! I raced downstairs to tell my parents of my new findings. Surely, this meant that I was not alone.

As I told them, my parents looked up at me in curiosity. "Are you sure there is no one else in our family who has it?" I asked. However, to the best of their knowledge, there wasn't. I thought further.

Maybe someone in the family does have Vitiligo. Maybe they're just hiding it from everyone, just as I plan to do.

I ran back upstairs to the computer, I wanted to know more. The internet connection, predictably, had failed, but after dialing up again, I noticed a different page had appeared. This was for a charity called the Vitiligo Society. The logo has not changed much over the years, and I recall how it vividly stood out, even then. I ran to get a pen, excited: *I need to get in touch here and see if someone can help me!*

Among some cursory information was a contact number, which I wrote down to follow up on. When I woke up the next morning and went down for breakfast, my head was pounding. I had been up all night with thoughts racing through my mind: about my treatment, what I would do during the year out from university, and how I would overcome this epic challenge alone.

If there was comfort, it was that the Vitiligo Society may have some suggestions. My parents were eagerly trying to talk to me that morning, but I avoided them: I think there was just too much on my mind. Instead, I wanted to call the Vitiligo Society immediately to get things going. I went for the phone, but then wondered if this was the route I wanted to take after all. I was just so confused and worried.

Then, clarity. I suddenly realised what I really needed was time. Specifically, time to take on board what I was putting my body through with the PUVA treatment. Gradually, the skin cancer risks started to dawn on me, and I questioned whether it was the right thing to do. I had to think this through. I was desperate, willing to try anything, but I could not just plunge into treatment without researching the risks.

Dad appeared to have been thinking along the same lines. Gently, he asked to speak to me, as I put away some dishes trying to avoid the discussion.

"Jot, are you sure this is what you really want to do about your skin?" Mum watched on.

"Yes, I think it is," I said assertively. I had made my mind up then and there: a day was more than enough for my decision and I had concluded there was nothing to lose by trying.

"Well, we will be right there by your side," replied Dad. That is how supportive my parents were: they did not want to see their daughter in pain, but what parent would? My family's support was the most important thing at that moment, because I knew I could rely on them heavily for guidance.

The start of my PUVA treatment and the start of my attempts to improve my Spanish coincided with each other. One September day, Mum had popped out to the local shops but had returned in an excitable mood.

"Look what I found!" she exclaimed, passing me a scribbled note. This turned out to be an ad for a Spanish lady who was offering home tutoring. At first it seemed like just a happy coincidence, but, unbeknownst to me at the time, this tutor would be a major influence in instilling confidence in my Spanish again.

I kept thinking of Sara and what she was doing – I missed her hugely. I just missed my best friend: our regular chats, seeing her face every day. Despite this, something inside me was quickly changing my feelings towards Sara. After one of the last conversations I had with her, as she embarked on her final year and I was at home, I began to reflect on things differently.

I need to let Sara go. I cannot be the same person I was in Spain. I am going through huge changes with my body, and how can anyone understand this? How would they ever understand? Sara is busy with finals now; she won't have time for me.

It was much easier for me to seal off that door and let Sara go and make new friends. What good was I to her? I started to feel sad, and I no longer wanted to speak to Sara because she didn't know what I was going through. Worse, I couldn't even explain it, because I didn't even know how I was feeling myself.

I started tutoring lessons with Carmen once a week. Carmen was a beautiful, older South American lady with a strong Spanish accent. At every session, her hair was neatly done up, and she would arrive at my house complete with matching handbags to her pristine outfits. I was always curious about whether she was married — she never really mentioned this —but I did discover that she had a son who lived with her.

Over the weeks, I gradually bonded with Carmen and got to know her better. She focused on my speaking and grammar, preparing interesting and authentic lessons that sparked my imagination and rebuilt my confidence. I loved her teaching approach, and to this day am grateful to her. Her positivity about my Spanish lifted me, and her lessons instilled so much self-confidence, which had been dented by my failure the year before.

Carmen was effusive with praise: *"Joti tienes buena pronunciación y vas a ser buena en español."* She believed in me, and she gave me the strength to push myself and excel in a subject I loved.

I continued with my Spanish lessons once a week, during which time I built a strong relationship with Carmen. She seemed to understand that I needed emotional support too. Sometimes, I was so drained from treatment that I would be exhausted during lessons, but she was always there by my side. I sometimes even think of her as a guardian angel, as if she knew what I was going through with my skin and could tell me with just a look. She had a deep understanding of my struggles without knowing the details. Most importantly, she was a source of support in a dark time when I had lost all sense of light.

King's College had sent instructions: which ward I was needed in and when. Mum wanted to come with me, but I felt I would be more comfortable alone.

I just need this time alone to think about things. I need to process what is going on.

The 68 bus took me to right outside the hospital.

This is it. I am here. There's no one to hold my hand now, but I chose it this way. I need to do this alone.

I managed to locate the correct dermatology ward and was greeted by a welcoming doctor, who sent me to the correct department for PUVA.

I was starting to feel on edge: *This is it, no turning back now...*

"I'm Dr. Hasmin, and I will be guiding you through your first course of PUVA treatment. Did you remember to take your Psoralen tablets two hours before coming today?"

"Yes," I replied. I had taken the pills straight after breakfast, but I'd felt sick afterwards. However, Dr. Hasmin reassured me that this was a common side effect of the tablets, and that this could happen quite often. While I despised how the tablets made me feel, I was eager to know more about my treatment.

I was told to take my clothes off, apart from my underwear, and then to stand in a cubicle of bright light for two minutes. Each week, I would increase the time spent in the light gradually to avoid burning my skin.

The first time in the cubicle, the treatment process felt manageable, but as weeks passed and the time increased, I began to feel exhausted. The bus journey to the hospital and back didn't help, and coupled with the sickness from the tablets, the treatment was mentally tiring. It just felt so long. Worse was to come.

One month into the light treatment, I suddenly started noticing more white Vitiligo patches on my right side. In fact, the one on my right arm appeared in the same place as my left arm. I was baffled by the symmetry: anyone would have thought that the spot on my left had been transferred to my right like a butterfly.

However, I continued with the PUVA routine for another eight weeks, and after the second month some of my pigment began to reappear. I was mystified, but elated: the PUVA was working!

I felt an immediate sense of relief and happiness, something I had not felt in a very long time. *I am going to be okay. I am going to be okay!*

It didn't last long. Soon, I would be thrown back into the deep end again.

Chapter 5 – Trapped in My Skin

"Things are never quite scary as when
you've got a best friend."
Bill Watterson[5]

I tried to remain positive with PUVA, especially because there were so few other treatment options available. When colour returned, I thought things may return to normal, but actually the opposite was true: my Vitiligo was spreading. Some days were more positive than others.

But as much as I had such a strong support network around me, no one could ever truly understand just how drained I was starting to feel. What I was going through and putting my body through was tough.

I could never work out the best way to consume the tablets, and I was always left feeling like I was on the verge of vomiting: an uncomfortable feeling to live with. Mum suggested different things to help, but I gradually started to feel resentment building towards the treatment process. My family just couldn't understand how destroyed I felt. Not only was I not completing my finals at university, but I was now alone; trapped inside my skin and my house, simply trying to cope with the physical and mental torture.

"Come downstairs and sit with us. Talk to me," Dad would often try to coax me out as I sheltered in my room, seeking solace in isolation. On reflection, this was the worst form of self-care, but I inflicted it upon myself because I was suppressing my thoughts and emotions, letting frustration build up inside.

Normally communicative, I was now struggling to get my words out and express myself: this was the unseen impact of Vitiligo on my world. I started to resent the condition, and I felt disgust towards it, like it was a parasite spreading to all areas of my body.

There was only one positive thing in my life at that time: my tutoring with Carmen. I longed for our weekly lessons, which distracted me and allowed my brain to reset. Above all, they reignited my passion for Spanish. Encouraged, I booked in more sessions with her, because I almost felt I needed some more distraction to counter the constant over-thinking about my skin. Carmen would prepare articles on South American literature, which I loved. She had a reassuring, calm voice and I felt really close to her.

Now and again, I checked the internet for any Vitiligo updates on Google. Yet the pages on the net remained the same, and there was never very much new information available. Eventually, I called the Vitiligo

Society, which turned out to be a huge turning point. As I sat by the family phone, looking at it, I wondered who would pick up and what advice they would have. I just wanted to speak to someone who knew what I was going through. Two rings. And then someone answered.

"Vitiligo Society, how can I help?"

I paused, unable to speak, my mind blank.

What do I say? How do I explain what has happened? Do I tell them the whole story about Spain or just what is going on now?

The lady had a soothing, understanding sort of voice, and told me to take my time and talk when ready. This gave me the courage to finally speak.

"I've just been diagnosed with Vitiligo. I saw your information on the internet so I thought I would call and find out more."

The lady from the society knew I was nervous, but she patiently described the work the charity did. She also mentioned a girl, Gurds, who was about the same age as me and had been trying to bring Vitiligo to the attention of the media. She also recommended I get in touch with a couple of other people.

Thoughts raced through my head. I wondered who the girl was, where she came from and how long she had suffered with Vitiligo. I was not even paying full attention to the lady by the end; I just wanted to get off the phone and call up Gurds.

Part of me did feel slightly uncomfortable at the thought of speaking to someone else with the condition, let alone another Asian girl of a similar age. Equally, I was happy to know that I was not alone with Vitiligo.

Could this be the start of a strong friendship? During our conversations around Vitiligo, maybe she'll be able to give me some advice and support?

I had felt so isolated up until this point, desperately seeking someone who was going through the same experiences as I was. So, without further hesitation, I called Gurds.

Within minutes, we were talking. She was sweet, telling me about her Vitiligo and her role in the Society. I wanted to know everything about her. It turned out that she'd had Vitiligo from a young age, and that she was from an Indian family too. I was shocked, but equally elated to have found her: we had the same ethos and understanding, which helped us connect and talk about our Vitiligo experiences for hours on end.

I needed to meet her. I wanted to see her in person and find out if she was real, because it all felt too good to be true. If I could meet someone who really understood what I was going through and how I was feeling, surely, I would be able to rely on her during this difficult time. She just seemed to have so much more confidence and understanding surrounding the condition than I did, which gave me hope for my own situation too.

Time went on. I started to get to know Gurds further, I continued with my tutoring, I gradually became more and more detached from my university friends, especially Sara. She was completing her final year and I knew she would be having the time of her life. I didn't want to bother her with tales of my misfortunes and figured she wouldn't understand anyway. Eventually, I lost all connection with Sara.

Now and again, she would call the house, but I told my parents to say I was not in. I just did not have the emotional capacity to explain how I was feeling. I wish

I hadn't taken this approach now, because I pushed away someone who could have helped me, but I chose to keep my distance because I was struggling. I couldn't accept or overcome the white patch, which was still spreading. At that time, distance was what I felt was best for me. Simultaneously, I was giving up hope with my PUVA treatment.

"PUVA didn't work for me," Gurds sighed. She explained in one of our conversations that she had also been through this and many other treatments. However, she was still keen to find out if there was still a possibility to reverse her skin. Like me, she did not want to have these white, unattractive patches all over her body.

We decided we had to work together and find a treatment, so after one of our conversations, Gurds and I decided to meet. It was almost like a first date: we had been speaking every week before deciding to meet in Central London.

Our meeting still counts as one of the most bizarre first encounters I have experienced. I hopped on the bus down to Brixton, then the Victoria Line tube to Oxford Circus. I hovered around nervously, until a petite, slim and dainty girl approached me. This had to be her.

As she got closer, I discreetly observed her appearance. Gurds was impeccably dressed, holding her handbag close to her chest. I was so nervous when she said my name, replying like a primary school child who was waiting to be called for an award in a school assembly.

"Oh great, I thought it was you," Gurds beamed. "Why don't we grab a coffee? I know a nice place around the corner."

"Sounds great!" I replied, as we walked side-by-side and chatted like we had known each other for years. I felt this sudden burst of happiness at meeting someone else with Vitiligo, but after a while, my voice sank to a murmur as I tried to hide my white spots with my long-sleeved coat. Even in Gurds' company, I felt such shame when showing my skin.

By this point, my Vitiligo had spread across my arms in patches, and it was also on my face, from my mouth to my eyes. I was finding it incredibly difficult to look directly at Gurds' Vitiligo too.

Is this what mine could become? This condition is so ugly, and I can't bear to look at it. But she's so beautiful. Maybe it's just about confidence.

I felt like I was looking at myself in the mirror, something I was already finding very hard to do. The condition was soul-destroying, and the more I looked at Gurds, I realised that I did not want my skin to look the same way. It was almost like seeing the future, which felt awfully difficult at the time.

Gurds and I chatted. As we did, I carefully observed the way she spoke and acted. She was sincere, so genuine and honest, and so beautifully made-up that she almost looked like a doll. Her skin was smooth and her Vitiligo patches blended in and out of her skin like a woven sheet. I wondered how she was able to carry herself in such a confident manner. Where did this confidence come from and how could she possibly let her Vitiligo be seen in public? This was an important question for me, because I never believed I would get to a stage of acceptance like Gurds: instead, treatment felt like my only option.

We talked about our families, our Sikh heritage and our upbringing. I thought about how our parents would get on too, because they were also from similar backgrounds. We talked about school and her experience with Vitiligo: Gurds had lived with it all her life, but she refused to be defined by it.

Most curiously, Gurds told me how she had written for magazines about her Vitiligo, and promised to show me the articles she'd written when I came to hers. I was astounded that she could write about her Vitiligo in such an open manner. Why would she want to show her Vitiligo off in front of anyone?

The conversation with Gurds made me realise I was trapped in my own skin. While I could not bear the thought of anyone looking at my skin, there Gurds was, appearing in big magazines like *Cosmopolitan*. I was curious to read the articles, and later I learned about the real difference she was making to others. In 1999, she was incredibly brave to talk publicly about the issue of Vitiligo acceptance.

Body positivity was not a movement then as it is now. There were no real figures in the media who represented Vitiligo or other visual differences and disabilities. Gurds was a real champion at that time, a hero to me, really. She was already educating people in magazines about her story, and I was hugely proud of her. I told her she was incredibly courageous to take a step like this, not just once, but multiple times across a range of publications.

Later, Gurds would ask me to take part in some campaigns too. She told me that the Vitiligo Society needed people like us to speak up, as they were always being approached by media outlets.

"No! No! There is absolutely no way I will be doing this, ever. I can't, no!" I was still too shy, sure that this was something I would never ever do or even contemplate doing at any stage of my life.

It had only been four months since my diagnosis, and I was not ready to start talking to my closest friends about Vitiligo, let alone the media. Gurds understood, and after a few drinks, it was time to go. How time had flown! It was so lovely to meet someone who shared my experiences that I wanted to talk to her all night long. We had a connection, a feeling of hope, and I knew that I needed her. She too, as someone who knew Vitiligo inside out, knew what I needed: a person who profoundly understood what Vitiligo was doing to my body.

Our friendship grew, and I would approach Gurds for everything and anything. She would be the one I would turn to when I noticed a new patch, or if I was struggling with patches appearing in more sensitive areas. It was not going to end here. I knew that we would be starting a new Vitiligo chapter together, and we did.

This closeness was not replicated at home. I had started to distance myself from my family. I knew they loved and cared for me, but they simply couldn't understand as well as Gurds. I didn't mean to hurt my family, but I became distant because I was suffering, hurting, and I felt truly vulnerable.

Elsewhere, I had stayed in touch with Nev, who I had got to know at university. We started to talk a lot more about my skin and what was going on. I never opened up to many people, but he took an interest in what was happening, which led to a connection and then to love. He was attentive and understanding, patient and kind. His sensitive nature made me feel secure and safe, and he became someone I could talk to when my anxiety peaked.

However, I needed to complete my finals, and this was my priority, so we remained just friends for a while. I also needed to get my brown skin back: I looked at it like an exam that could be passed with hard work and dedication, but this wasn't really the case.

Still, I felt suffocated within my own body. A white, ugly monster was growing on the outside of me, and I quickly became a recluse. The only people I would speak to were Nev, Gurds and occasionally my family, but I remained distant because it was the only way I could cope.

I felt stripped of my freedom to wear what I wanted. My patches were spreading and, conversely, my personality was slowly being stripped away. This autoimmune condition may not have been killing me physically, but mentally I was being crushed.

Chapter 6 – Hiding from The World

"We cannot forever hide the truth
about ourselves, from ourselves."
John McCain[6]

Alone in isolation, I started to conceal my pain and frustration by cutting off from the real world. It was the only way I could deal with the Vitiligo. The white plague spread across my body, and there was not a minute in the day I would not spend thinking about how I could get things under control.

I spent days and weeks and months living on edge. I was nervous, tense and worried all the time, and I realised that I was starting to suffer with anxiety. This would peak at family functions, if I needed to be out in public, or if we went to our local *Gurdwara*. Vitiligo had made its way into my temple of peace. I felt it growing, and I could not control or restrain it.

This is a place I feel at home. This is a place of calm and peace. Why am I feeling such tension at a place of worship, where I have always felt comfortable and secure?

The following morning, I woke to the smell of my mother's home cooking. My bedroom was directly above the kitchen, and the aromas were tantalizing. I longed for my mothers' fresh *prantas*, and even though I felt sluggish, her cooking encouraged me to rise out of bed.

Most mornings, I would take my time with this. I did not have a structured early morning routine. I justified my long hours of sleep with the notion that I was carrying my skin as a burden. I felt exhausted all the time, which in turn made me feel like hiding under my duvet for longer than normal. I was conscious that I was becoming despondent about my skin, as well as the deeper effect on my confidence. I was continuously thinking about Vitiligo, and I did not realise just how fatigued I was starting to feel.

This morning was worse than normal, because we had just got an invitation to my cousin Rajvir's* wedding, happening in a few weeks. I was happy for her and I wanted to be there for her wedding, but I could not dress up and smile when I was mentally all over the place.

I am not going to that wedding. How can I? What is going to happen there? How can I cover up my skin without people gawping at me? I do not have the energy nor the willpower to talk about it. I am not going!

*Name has been changed to protect identity

I made my way downstairs and heard my parents discussing the venue and timings of the wedding. I came down and glared at them.

"Dad, I'm not going. I can't. What am I going to wear?" I asked, becoming hysterical. Mum came over too, and they took a moment to respond.

"Jot, we will find a way. We still have a few weeks until the day, so we have some time to think about it."

Dad always had a smooth and calm manner about him, which made it easier to approach him and discuss things. I knew my parents were hurting, and I did not want to cause them any further stress, so I tried my best to think logically and find a way around the wedding. I did not want to attend, but it was a difficult situation: this was a first cousin and my absence would be hard to justify to others.

This is the reality of being South Asian, you are judged or frowned upon for many reasons, especially if you are not perceived as slim, fair-skinned and long-haired, if you do not have a good degree. The list can go on and on: how others perceive you is crucial.

The Mojatu Foundation[7] confirms on their website that a huge number of British Asians suffer from mental health problems, but many refuse help because they worry about what others will say or think. The need to preserve family reputation can override mental health issues, happiness and a person's wellbeing.

I have met many South Asian women who feel under pressure to fit into society's norms, even without a skin condition. Now that I had Vitiligo, where exactly did I fit in with such a community? I was torturing myself, thoughts flooding my head, and the more I stressed, the more my Vitiligo spread. I would see a patch on the right side of my body, then the same spot on the left a few days later. Every time I saw a new pigment on my body, I knew what was to follow: the same mark on the other side.

It was all very symmetrical, which led to the feeling that Vitiligo was ruling me, taking me over from head to toe. My family tried their best to help me, but how can you support someone when you haven't been through it yourself? The only person who understood was Gurds, and we grew ever closer.

I decided she was the only person that would be able to help me with the wedding problem. I called her straight away: I don't even think I stopped to ask her how she was before explaining the issue. I blurted out that we had a family wedding to go to, how I felt such pressure about what to wear. I told her the wedding was in five weeks, but that I did not have a clue about how I would cover-up my Vitiligo. I broke down crying.

"I don't want to look like the ugly duckling," I sobbed, tears rolling down my cheeks. I was so upset that I did not even hear her response. However, Gurds was calm and her voice was as smooth as silk. Eventually, she got through to me.

"Joti, don't worry about it, there are plenty of long-sleeved suits in Southall, let's go shopping together. I'll help you find something."

I continued crying, but I felt some relief at the thought that Gurds could help me blend in, or at least not draw any attention to myself. I took deep breaths as I realised there could be a solution, and a few days later, we arranged a date to meet in Southall.

"Why not short-sleeved? We have some new ones in fashion that have just come out. Why don't you take a look?" the shop assistant stared at me up and down. I felt like she could see my Vitiligo through my clothing, and I instantly took a dislike to her.

Did she not hear me clearly? I said long-sleeved. Do I really need to tell her why I don't need a short-sleeved suit? Why can't she just understand?

Gurds looked back and forth between me and the shop assistant, before telling her that it was just long-sleeved suits we were interested in.

"I want to get out of here," I whispered to Gurds, "I do not like the look of this place and how she is making me feel."

"Joti, listen. We're here now. Let's just take a quick look." She reassured me that if we didn't see anything straight away, we would leave. I felt safe with Gurds, and I knew she had a rational way of thinking. And so I agreed to stay and have a look around.

I remember the shop assistant. The skin on her arms was loose and flapped like huge fleshy wings. Surely, she of all people could understand why I'd want a long-sleeved top? I could not help but feel a little anger towards her. She showed us several designs and, each time she appeared with a new outfit, I felt disappointed. The suits were not contemporary, made for someone twice my age. Nothing looked elegant, and as we left the shop, I could only see mannequins with sleeveless outfits. Not one had a long-sleeved top. I started to lose hope, unsure if I wanted to continue.

But we did. Gurds took me to all the shops on the Broadway, and by the end of the day, we had been everywhere. However, as we went from one shop to another, I became downhearted. Were there no Indian suits that would cover my skin in the way I wanted them to? How would I ever find something that makes me feel comfortable? We must have spent at least eight hours in the shops and markets before we finally entered one shop and I saw a suit I loved.

"It has to be long-sleeved," I told the man, who was tall, thin and stood straight-backed like a soldier. It had been a long day, and I needed him to give me the answer I needed. A solution. I was desperate now.

"We can sew sleeves onto the suit. Would that be something you would like us to do?" he smiled. My eyes lit up as I looked at Gurds. It was not the ideal solution, but it was something I could do to cover up my skin and it could possibly work. I wondered why I hadn't thought of it myself.

I didn't even ask the price, as I knew I would pay whatever was needed to have a suit I liked with long sleeves. I was also drained by this point, so I wasn't even fussed about the effect adding them on would have. It would have sleeves and that was all I needed to know.

It took two hours to complete, and we returned a short time later to collect the finished product. This was a good time to sit down and eat something, as it was already dinner time, so I called my parents to let them know I would be having dinner with Gurds in Southall. I told Dad that I'd finally found a solution, and he sounded relieved. Not only that I had found something to wear for the wedding, but that I would be attending. He wouldn't have to explain my absence, so me finding a suit was a huge relief for my parents too!

Gurds and I were famished. We found an old-looking *dhaba*-type place and sat down to order some snacks. A *dhaba* in India is a roadside food stall, but the place in Southall was more like a restaurant, authentically decorated inside. Food was served on a *thali*, a traditional metal plate.

I was exhausted and could not really think straight. Gurds and I talked the whole experience over, and she told me how she had started going to weddings wearing sleeveless clothing now. She no longer felt the need to rely on long sleeves to cover up her skin.

"You know Joti, I wasn't always as confident as I am now," she told me. She shared how her life had been growing up with Vitiligo, and I learned, like me, that she was the only one with the condition in her family.

"Is it going to have to be like this every time I have a family function?" I asked, fatigue in my voice. "I can't do this." The shopping trip had not only been physically exhausting but mentally draining too.

The more I learned about Gurds, the more I realised that she was a strong and confident woman who did not allow her skin to take over her life. I felt this was the opposite of myself. Inside, I wondered whether she was confident because she'd had more time to accept her skin: surely if you'd had a condition from a young age, your outlook would be different than if you were diagnosed later in life? I thought so.

While I had my own theories about Gurds' feelings about her skin, I know she battled with it too. Her evolving skin was a struggle for her as it was for me, but the more time I spent with her, the more I knew I would never accept the condition like she did. I felt I would never get to a place of positive thinking about Vitiligo. This disease was negatively impacting my life, and I was certain there was nothing I could do to change my attitude. Or so I thought!

That evening, when I arrived home, my parents had left me a note to say they were popping out to get some dinner. I was so tired, all I wanted to do was go straight to sleep, so I was relieved not to have to recant the whole shopping experience. My chat with Gurds about self-acceptance resonated with me. I could not help but think about what Vitiligo was going to do to me: it was already starting to destroy my life, and no matter how much support I had, I could not let these negative thoughts go. Before I could sleep, Nev called me, and we spoke briefly about my whole experience.

"I don't know why you want to cover yourself up," he told me, "You are beautiful as you are."

Why is he being so nice to me? Am I falling in love? Is this what love is supposed to feel like?

It certainly felt like it. He was by my side through all of this, and a connection was growing. I had someone who I could tell was there for me and felt stronger than anything I had experienced with anyone else. I went to bed with emotions flying around my head. Finally, I drifted off into a deep sleep, trying to understand what was happening to me and the world around me.

Chapter 7 – Finals, the Finale!

"Ability is what you're capable of doing.
Motivation determines what you do.
Attitude determines how well you do it."
Lou Holtz[8]

Months passed by. Nev and I met as friends, but it was developing into what felt like something more. Although I was not physically ready to take on a relationship, it felt uplifting to have someone who was interested in my condition and wanted to support me.

Nev was different from everyone else. He showed he cared and he was genuine about his feelings. He started to open up to me and express how he felt, but I had a lot on my plate at the time. I realised the most important thing for me at this time was my final year at university: nothing and no one was going to get in my way.

If I mess this up again, there is no going back.

I remained focused and driven, so I kept Nev at a friendship level. This was increasingly difficult for me, but it was necessary if I was to finish my finals and complete my degree. With December approaching, I was excited by illuminations and the festive season getting closer: a little joy that was probably the first time I had felt some sort of happiness in a long time. Butterflies were fluttering around my stomach, and I wondered if this had anything to do with my feelings for Nev. However, I left it there and I just carried on as normal.

Christmas passed, and while I was taking down the tree that year, I remember reflecting on how much time I had spent on PUVA treatment since September. I look back and realise the year out of university was a blessing in disguise, because I was able to spend time on "fixing my Vitiligo".

I had persevered with the treatment and was eager to see my skin turn brown again. Part of me had even hoped I'd have pigment back before I started term again the following September. Small speckles, brown dots had started to appear on some parts of my body, which I first noticed on my legs. When I saw the very first pigment reappear, a huge wave of excitement rushed through my body, a sign that everything was going to be ok.

"Let's have a look," my family asked, curiously, when I told them. There was a sense of shock and surprise, almost as if they were not expecting this to happen.

PUVA treatment was a very tough process to go through: I would have to organise my routine around the sessions, which meant I was not as free as I wanted to be.

My family did their best to support me at this difficult time, mostly by cooking nutritious meals. Mum would always try her best to ensure that I was staying healthy, and I always had a good variety of green vegetables on my plate. I listened to the advice people gave, and I ate the food Mum cooked. However, the hardest part, six months on from being diagnosed, was that my Vitiligo was still being kept secret from the rest of the world.

From January onwards, I only had five months remaining before my final exams. This was an important time for me, and I could not afford to mess up, so I continued with my tutoring with Carmen and thrived during these lessons.

My exam date finally arrived, and I was invited to sit the exams at the faculty of languages at Queen Mary's. Getting on the train and approaching the University made me feel very nervous: not only did I have my exams to sit, but I wanted to avoid everybody I knew who was on the same course as myself. I felt embarrassed, and I did not want anyone to spot me.

This would mean explaining my Vitiligo, and I was not ready to share this with anyone just yet.

While vulnerable, I was also feeling incredibly confident with my subject knowledge. Deep inside, I knew that everything I worked for was going to be fine. I had devoted all my time and energy towards my degree, I knew that I had done the best I could.

The year had passed by quickly, and I was eager to receive my results. It was an almost immediate response: two days later I received a phone call from Ester, my tutor since the first year of university.

"Joti, is that you?"

"Yes, it is."

"I wanted to say, all your hard work has paid off and you have passed your exam. You'll be going forward to your finals in September. Well done."

My heart was pounding. I wanted to scream. This was the happiest I had felt in such a long time, and I wanted the world to know how I was feeling: I wanted to share my happiness with everyone. This was the news I had been waiting on for months; that I was going to make it into my final year at university.

First, I had to call home. My parents deserved to know first, as they had supported me all along. I called Dad and shared the good news with him. He was elated, and I felt a huge weight lifted off my shoulders. I then spoke to my Mum. She was so relieved and happy for me.

I then was left with one very important person to call, Carmen. She had been so supportive, and although she was about 40-years older than me, she had become my best friend during that year. She helped boost my confidence and taught me a lot about South American history through her tutoring sessions. I loved the time that I spent with her and I knew I would truly miss it, just sitting there listening to her gentle voice explaining grammar and history to me. She instilled an abundance of confidence in me, and I knew she would never know how grateful I was to her for giving me such encouragement.

I really believe in the power of words. Through all my years of teaching and working with people, I've found that there are ways to express yourself and say how you feel without hurting the people you care about. Carmen helped me understand this: she knew that I had a huge hurdle to pass, but she was so kind to me and stayed positive throughout.

I did, however, start to wonder about Sara and the friends she had made in her final year. I was feeling guilty at this point, as I had not been in touch with her, often ignoring her calls. I missed her friendship and was revisited by all the memories that we had shared together.

Even though I should have remained positive, I could not be fully happy. I knew that my finals would not be the same, and I knew that my final year would be very different to how life had been with Sara.

The beautiful, autumnal September Monday morning could not have arrived sooner. The front door was slightly ajar with my suitcases, all ready and packed to leave. "We are going to miss you Jot," Dad said as I grabbed his car keys. I knew I had one chance at this, and I was grateful for every moment. I had been packing weeks in advance for my final year at university, and I was so excited at the thought of completing my finals. I just wanted to slip out of the door, but then remembered that dad would be taking me to my university digs.

"Work hard and do your best," he said as he left me. I was left in a beautiful, polished apartment, which had my own sink and wardrobe. There were five of us living in this student block, and we immediately introduced ourselves. Everyone was very private, and I soon learned that there would be no real communication here. Everyone took their finals seriously from the start.

Maybe this is the environment I need. No parties, no wasting time, no long chit chats. Just serious people.

After spending four hours unpacking, I started to feel at home and decided to have an early night. Freshers' night. I started to make my way around the campus, reminding myself of what the university looked like. As I took some steps, I breathed in the smell of each modern university building. It felt like I had never been away from university at all. There were students everywhere, some taking suitcases out, some wheeling them to their blocks, and others giving their families the strongest hugs I had ever seen. I walked around campus. My block was right opposite my faculty, and I thought there'd be at least one person I would recognize, but there was no one I knew. I decided to head back to my room and make myself something to eat.

I headed straight to the kitchen, prepared a little sandwich and gazed out of the window, wondering what type of year I was going to have.

I do not want loads of friends. I do not feel interested in this. I just want to meet a person I trust, so we can support one another with our course if we need to.

Then, I met Rita*, an Indian girl with long curly locks. When she spoke, her words floated out of her mouth as she spoke in a soft, feathery whisper. She was kind and sincere and told me she was studying French. I remember thinking how great it was to find another Asian girl studying languages, as there were not many of us on the course.

"A few of us are going to the freshers party. Would you like to come with us?" she asked.

"I would love to!" I responded, overjoyed. This was one of the few events we attended together, and I did not initially think we would end up so close. However, we did, and I was grateful I met her as she helped me ease back into university life. Above all, she encouraged me to start meeting people again.

I also kept in touch with Nev, as friends, and now and again we would meet up in London and spend time together. We talked about university and my skin.

*Name has been changed to protect identity

I realised I was falling for him a little more each time. He was always there for me. However, I was not yet prepared to take things any further. I wanted to be friends and just focus on my finals.

His kindness made me reflect on my future plans. As I started trusting him more and more, I realised he was the first friend who had really supported me with my continuously-changing skin.

I had invested a lot of time completing the treatment, and in total I probably spent around 10 months at King's. I knew I had to continue with the treatment, so when I entered my finals, I was pleased when my GP told me to continue my treatment at Whitechapel Hospital instead, which was closer to my university. I was still keen to find out if PUVA would fully work for me, because this was my only hope of ever getting my pigment back.

After just three months, I decided I was unable to continue with the treatment. Although the hospital was not too far from my university accommodation, the bus trip to Whitechapel made me feel very uneasy.

Whitechapel was very different to South London, and I would notice people staring at me, which made me feel uncomfortable. This was a predominantly Muslim area, and most women would only be seen with their husbands and children. I did not feel comfortable on my own in the area, nor did I feel comfortable at the hospital, which did not have the warmth that I had established at King's. At the same time, I noticed my Vitiligo patches spreading, and I started to realise that perhaps this was not the right treatment for me, especially in finals year.

So, I gave it up. I did not even think twice, and I never went back to PUVA treatment. Sometimes I wonder: If I were not under such pressure, would PUVA have worked? Regardless, I was not concerned about stopping treatment, although I did wonder what I was going to do next.

I had settled very well into my final year, and as I focused on my education, weeks turned into months, and very quickly December was around the corner. I had already completed half a year, and I was happy to be focusing my energy into working as hard as I could at university.

However, there was a problem. Rita and I were to attend a student event, and she had asked me to come over to her place to get ready. We were both very focused, and she seemed to have the same aspirations and goals as myself, but it was an agonizing situation.

How do I get around this? I cannot let her see my patches or my skin. What will she think of me? What if she does not want to hang out with me? What if she refuses to be my friend because of this? This condition is way too ugly. I cannot let anyone see it. It is easier to cover this up. There must be a way of covering this up.

This is when I started to investigate and look at ways of covering up my skin. I remember taking myself to the university library, then discreetly getting a corner booth so I could research makeup to cover up my Vitiligo on the internet.

My Vitiligo was spreading, and I needed something that would hide it. I stayed in touch with Gurds, and halfway through my finals, I decided to give her a call from the landline in my university block. She was happy to hear my voice, and we just started chatting.

During our conversation I told her that my Vitiligo was spreading, and she immediately suggested that I try Charles Fox camouflage makeup in Covent Garden. She told me that this makeup was used for actresses and actors in theatrical performances: this could work for the extensive patches I wanted to hide.

That same day, I made an appointment to go down to Charles Fox and see if they could color match their makeup with my skin. Excitement grew as I made my way to Covent Garden: I had realised that if this makeup worked, it could solve a lot of problems. I was not ready to explain to anyone what I had. I was not sure if this condition was going to go away, and I was not in the right frame of mind to start talking about my skin, especially when I wanted to focus on my final year at university.

A young, kind lady directed me to where she would be testing and trialing out some products on my skin. In full makeup, she directed me to where we would go for my colour match, but when I showed her my extensive Vitiligo, she drew her eyebrows together and turned her mouth down in a look of concern.

"We may not be able to get an exact color match to skin. You have different shades of Vitiligo and pigment all over your body, but we will try our best."

The lady spent three or so hours showing me how to apply the product. First with a sponge all over, then a fixing spray to seal it, then fixing powder to set the make-up. For me, this was a revelation. I had never seen anything like this before, and it was the first time I'd used camouflage makeup for my Vitiligo. I thought this would be the solution to hiding my Vitiligo from the rest of the world, and it did work for me for the duration of my finals.

I spent a fortune on makeup camouflage products from Charles Fox for the next four years. Every time I would attend a function or student party, I felt I could cover up by using these products, which allowed me to fit in and not feel like I stood out from the crowd. I kept my skin hidden and was determined on working towards my final year at university, rather than using all that energy to look at any new patches that would appear on my skin.

This was how I completed my course. I shifted my mindset towards my final year modules and really focused on those units, rather than looking at every aspect of my skin every minute of the day.

Then, one day, I decided to pack Vitiligo up in a box and pop it firmly under the bed in my mind. I thought this would work; if I could just forget about it, then it would just disappear.

However, this was an illusion. I would quickly find out that nothing I could do would erase this condition from my life…

Chapter 8 – Torturing Myself

"You may feel powerless as a child but the world one day will be yours and you are responsible for it. So, seize the day and take charge of it."
Harvey Fierstein[9]

"I got the job!"

I yelled at Dad when I told him. I would now be working in Canary Wharf at Barclays Corporate, my dream job. I just had this feeling that corporate banking would be the job I would stay in for a lifetime. My long-term goal was to work in international banking and travel the world.

Shortly after I received my starter pack, I immediately started working in the city. However, this brings a certain pressure to look and dress a certain way. It was great in so many aspects though: I loved the buzz and the drive it gave me, and the commutes were always entertaining. I loved to observe people on the trains and buses, gaining inspiration from the latest clothing women wore in this chic part of London.

However, there was huge discomfort on the trains too. The hot, stuffy underground in summer was unbearable and reminded me how I felt imprisoned in my own skin, unable to take off my jacket or wear sleeveless clothing like everyone else. It was torturous and I was isolated because of the way that I dressed. I felt like people judged me: maybe they thought I wore this clothing for religious reasons. The result was hours and hours spent searching for perfect long-sleeved tops while using makeup as my shield.

Finding long-sleeved clothing during the peak of summer was not easy at all. I had to prepare myself weeks in advance and hunt around for garments that would conceal every spot of my Vitiligo. I would enter shops, hopeful I would find the perfect top, but most of the time I left feeling deflated and confused, wondering how I would get through the commutes and the hot summer months. It was an incredibly difficult process.

Canary Wharf is almost like a mini-London, compactly pressed into a small space. It has glistening shiny floors, an abundance of takeaway restaurants and every designer shop you can think of. There were some high street shops there too though, so it was really the perfect place for any shopper. Apart from me, apparently: you would have thought I'd have been able to select at least a few items of clothing, but this was far from the case.

Often, I would get glances from people commuting and I just knew what they were thinking: *Isn't she hot in that?* Inside the offices it was different: they were fully air-conditioned and most people wore a blazer or jacket at work, so I did not feel like I stood out as much. This type of environment worked fine for me, and I could almost get away with wearing long-sleeved clothing, but outside of the office I panicked about what to wear.

I had to plan my outfits long in advance: for work and for family events. It felt excessive. I was overthinking, over-worrying, spending my lunch breaks searching for appropriate outfits just to look normal. My priority was to at least cover my skin so I would not draw any unnecessary attention to myself.

Planning was an essential part of my routine. I know people plan things every day of their lives, but when it came down to planning weeks in advance for a party or wedding, I knew my anxiety was getting worse. It even got to the point that I planned all my outfits for work a week beforehand, so I didn't have to decide what to wear each morning. I already had enough on my plate with my makeup and did not need any additional pressure. Ultimately, I just wanted to look the same as everyone else and not be seen as different.

The pressure was immense to conform to society's norms and "fit in."

Canary Wharf was not a long commute from where my parents lived, but the role at Barclays was short-lived. I realised that the sales role within the corporate sector did not represent my personal values, so I left after eight months to do some temping work in the city. I worked for a variety of different international banks, Citigroup, BNP Paribas, Bank of New York and Credit Suisse, which was a wonderful opportunity because it gave me an insight into the industry. I also loved the fact that, because I was on a short-term contract, no one had time to get to know about my skin condition. This was a huge weight off my shoulders.

City life is interesting because people place so much importance on looks. Men and women would be suited and booted, and you would never see anyone with a hair out of place. The corporate clothing look was elegant and appealed to me, but in the end it was unachievable. In the hot summer months, I was unable to wear skirts and sleeveless tops. I would find myself travelling on the London Underground in long-sleeve clothing, hiding my skin from the world. It was difficult to continue this way, but I felt I had no choice at that time. This was the safest option.

My Vitiligo had spread like wildfire and, at this point, I now had patches on my arms, legs, face, chest and neck. While I could just about handle the Vitiligo on the rest of my body, my chest was a bridge too far. I remember seeing the first patch on my right breast and feeling absolutely mortified. I spent hours and hours thinking the same thoughts, mentally torturing myself into an emotional wreck.

Why can I not look the same as everyone else? Why is this happening to me? Why is this still spreading?

My family stepped in and sat down with me several times, telling me that I needed to reduce my stress levels. This, apparently, would help slow the spread. As much as I tried, I just could not seem to reduce my anxiety. In fact, anxiety overtook my worries about Vitiligo by the end.

My morning routine, just to get to "normal" was exhausting.

06:00. Wake up.
06:15. Brush my teeth.
06.30. Start applying my derma blend makeup. Start with the cream all over my body, including arms, hands and face and feet if I was wearing stilettos.
07:15. Apply the fixing spray.

07:30. Apply the fixing powder.
07:45. Quick breakfast.
08:00. Leave for work.

My routine stayed the same every day, but I was starting to tire of it. Yet, I had no choice and I had to keep going. What other option did I have? I had to ensure that my Vitiligo was fully concealed on every part of my body. What was the point in wearing camouflage if people could see my pigment? I needed to cover up so no one saw a thing. I continued with camouflage makeup for a good while, and this was how I survived, my only acceptance.

Gurds was always there for me. We would speak from time to time, and she would share some of her ideas about clothing, but I was struggling. I felt like I had withered away inside like a dead flower. My temping jobs stopped, but I then found a more permanent role working as a PA at a company called Gartmore in Tower Hill. I fell in love with the firm, where I worked with the kindest and most lovely people, including a wonderful boss who really supported me when I joined. However, I often wondered how I ended up on the PA career path. I especially missed speaking Spanish, so I thought about how I could incorporate this into my working life. Then, one day, I bumped into an old friend from high school, Dominique, on the way home from work. After some small talk, I told her I was missing using my Spanish in the city.

"Why don't you tutor my mum in Spanish? She would love it and it would also give her company," she said.

I loved the idea, and I was pleased to have the chance to speak Spanish again. I did feel some sense of loss at being unable to use my language skills in banking.

Without hesitation, I told Dominique to tell her mum that I would tutor her, and before long I had set up some lessons with Karen, a beautiful Anglo-Indian lady with dark short hair that was always perfectly styled. She was sophisticated in the way she spoke, and she always called me "*Joti beta*", meaning Joti darling, which was lovely. She had been brought up in India and would always humour me with her Punjabi pronunciation of phrases. I loved working with Karen, and she thoroughly enjoyed the lessons too.

One day, she said something to me that inspired my next career move. I was in the middle of teaching the grammar rule of "*ser*" and "*estar*". These are two important verbs for "to be" in Spanish, but are used in different contexts. Sometimes this can be more challenging for English-speakers, because we only have one verb "to be", but Karen seemed to grasp when both verbs are used and in which contexts. We started to drill the verbs, practicing them aloud. As I continued to explain the differences, I saw a puzzled look on her face as she stared at me. I knew she wanted to ask me something, but I was not sure what.

Oh dear. She doesn't understand. Am I moving too quickly? Does she find my approach too slow? Perhaps I ought to ask her.

Karen smiled. "Joti," she started, "Can I just say, I think you would be great as a teacher. You must look into it; you would be wonderful. Think about all the students' lives you could change for the better with your passion for languages!" She shone with happiness as she continued, "Never have regrets. Follow your heart and do what makes you happy." Her words never left me and remain in my heart today.

We had the conversation several times and, as I left her house each week, I started to feel more comfortable, even excited with the idea of pursuing a teaching career. I decided to offer tutoring to some more students by word of mouth, and eventually I had four students per week. While it was tiring after my long day in the city, I realised I was falling in love with teaching.

I'm going to do it.

I smiled confidently as I entered Karen's house for our final lesson. She grabbed me and gave me the biggest hug, telling me that I would make it and become an outstanding teacher. Before making the big decision to do the PGCE qualification, I thought I'd try out the Certificate of Language Teaching to Adults (CELTA) first. I called up a few places and applied to a course at Goldsmiths University. It was perfect, because evening classes for adults would fit in nicely with my schedule.

In January 2004, I continued working in the city, tutoring, and completing the CELTA course. Meanwhile, my Vitiligo was spreading. Sometimes I felt content with the plans I was making, other times I was lost in a dark, sad world. I still felt no one could understand what my body was going through. However, one person stayed at my side: Nev.

He seemed to appear when I was at my lowest points, lifting me with his positivity when times were dark. We would meet up now and again in the city and just talk. He seemed to understand my experience, to the point that it felt like he had Vitiligo himself sometimes. He just demonstrated this deeper level of understanding and empathy.

By 2004, we both knew that there was a growing love between us, and I finally decided I wanted to share this news with my parents. I was constantly evolving, changing, and not just my skin. While I was hiding this from the world, there was one person seeing it all, who accepted me for me. I knew this was deeper, more special than anything I had ever experienced before. I knew I could not let him go.

"I want us to get married," he told me one evening. He looked into my eyes as he told me that he wanted to spend the rest of his life with me. "The colour of your skin is not important to me. You are. I want us to have a future together, regardless of your Vitiligo."

I made my decision instantly. At 26, I had found the life partner I wanted. I wanted to be loved, to feel pretty, and to get married to someone I loved too. He made me feel all of this and more: I had never experienced love like it before. This wasn't a love based on looks, but something far deeper. If he loved me for my brown skin and my white spots, I felt sure it was a true, honest, genuine love.

All that was left to do was share the news with my family…

Chapter 9 – Getting Hitched

"Marry someone who loves you entirely for you,
as marriage is so much more than being skin-deep."
Joti Gata-Aura

"Get married? To whom?"

My parents looked at me in despair as I broke the news to them. I knew it was not going to be the easiest conversation: I had always been very close to my parents, to the extent that I had never dated anyone and always thought they would end up introducing me to my future partner. With my changing skin and insecurities, I even thought it might be best. I already felt very vulnerable and did not want the added pressure of a boy judging me. Nev was different though, as I tried to explain.

"I just know that Nev is the right partner for me," I went on, not giving them a word in edgeways. I wanted to prove that I had met someone loving and decent, from a good family background with solid values. That was more important than anything else.

It took a further two years for us to decide on the wedding date. It was the most exciting time of my life, but it was marred by my skin becoming even whiter and my growing anxiety about it. The overwhelming occasion of the wedding was starting to worry me greatly.

As the days and weeks passed, I grew increasingly nervous, and tension flowed through my body like a rough wave, pushing me from side to side, jerking me at every stage. I did not feel I had the capacity to hide my skin, but I also had no other option. No one could be allowed to see my Vitiligo, no one even knew it was there. There was no discussion on body image, so why start talking about this now?

I decided my best option was to continue to keep things hidden. It was a secret I would keep to myself for the next 20 years, so I was certainly not prepared to look ugly and be judged by all the aunties and uncles on my big wedding day.

Coming from the Indian culture is challenging. There is so much pressure to look a certain way and, over centuries, women have been conditioned to behave accordingly. This is what life was like and why I believed that my skin was an embarrassment.

"Kini soni hai," the aunties and uncles would say when you were dressed up looking perfect at family events. Looking the part was part of culture, and if you did

not, then you simply did not fit in. *"Kini soni hai,"* meant how beautiful you look and was a phrase constantly used at weddings.

I always wondered why there was such pressure. In the months leading up to my wedding, I thought about what I would wear and how I could cover my skin. With 500 people looking at me, surely someone would spot my Vitiligo eventually. As soon as an aunty had clocked it, the gossip would spread like wildfire. I almost had nightmares about the scenario, then started to lose my appetite fearing the worst: *What would happen if someone saw?*

I imagined people taking photos and the light shining on the one part of my skin that would reveal my secret. Someone holding my hand or hugging me, then wiping the makeup off. All sorts of things came into my head and I really started to panic: what should have been a happy time for me was the most anxious, stressful time I ever experienced.

One evening, Mum and Dad sat me down over dinner to ask what I wanted to do about the *chunni and mayian* ceremonies. *Chunni* is a pre-wedding event, where the girls get together and celebrate with food and music. Dad suggested we host it at home, a few days before the wedding. I, however, was not keen.

"I'm not doing it. I am not letting anyone touch my skin. I don't want it, and that is that." I snapped, and Dad looked dismayed. He tried to convince me it was part of our culture and seemed worried about what people would say.

"I don't know, Dad. I just can't have anyone lifting my sleeves and doing things to my arms and legs. They are bound to see my Vitiligo." I started crying, because I knew how important it was for Mum especially, but also because I wanted to take part in this important ceremony too. I just couldn't. Dad looked down. He understood my worries and decided to stop the conversation at that point.

The *mayian* was another concern. Generally considered a fun part of the pre-wedding function, it consists of the bride's mother and aunts rubbing a paste of turmeric, flour and mustard oil onto her face, arms, and legs. Meanwhile, they sing traditional songs. The belief is that this cleanses and balances the body for married life. I felt deflated: *I am missing part of my own wedding ceremony because of my Vitiligo. This is taking over my life.*

Eventually, I agreed to a compromise: Mum and one of my aunts would complete the ceremony on my hands only. However, I was fearful that when the yellow paste was applied, it would take off my Dermablend camouflage. People would spot my patches and, by then, it would be too late. Everyone would know about my white, patchy, uneven and discolored skin. The thought of this made me feel physically sick.

I was confused and did not know what to do, so I decided to sleep on it. While I should have been thinking about my outfits and enjoying the whole experience, I felt so trapped within my own skin. The conversation had left me emotionally drained.

Mum was cooking *prantas* on the stove the next morning. She told me that just a little of the ritual on my hands would be fine, as it was an important part of the wedding, and I saw the relief on her face when I agreed. I was still very unsure, because I was sure the aunties would jump in and carry out the same ritual on other parts of my skin too. After all, this was a very religious part of the wedding.

I was now in full swing with wedding preparations. But I now had the next hurdle to overcome: finding a makeup artist. Indian artists cost a fortune, and I needed one who would not only make me feel very special on the day, but would be able to conceal my Vitiligo too.

Luckily, I was recommended a well-respected makeup artist Rivaaz*, and Gurds had also heard of her, so I felt a bit more confident, even if I felt nervous talking to someone about my skin condition. I was embarrassed and unsure how to approach the issue.

Would she have seen Vitiligo before? Would she know how to cover up my skin? How would she blend my patches?

I called Rivaaz up the next day and we spoke at length about what sort of look I wanted. She then suggested I book a trial, so a few weeks later, I went down to see her. We were greeted by a plump woman with a big, warm smile across her face. She seemed kind and caring and already knew my story. Through her eyes, I could see that she wanted to help, which made me happy with the decision I'd made.

When a bride gets married, it is always a difficult process, but Vitiligo made the planning and preparation even harder. Despite this, I continued to plough forward the best I could. Some days would be filled with happiness at moving onto the next stage of my life, but on others, I felt true sorrow for the skin I was losing and the person I was leaving behind.

*Name has been changed to protect identity

The big day came around so quickly. I could not believe how the months had flown by, and now the day was here. I had to get myself up at 5 a.m. to get my makeup done, as it would take me five hours to get ready and dressed into my bridal outfit. This was what I had planned: a red *lengha* (embroidered skirt) and a long-sleeved top with a red veil that draped over the whole outfit. I had seen so many pictures in wedding magazines of brides adorned in gold-embroidered clothing, with beautifully-done hair and flawless makeup. I wanted to look like this, to feel special, so I worked closely with a designer who came highly recommended.

I knew my dress would be different, because it would need to cover up my Vitiligo, but I always dressed quite modestly anyway. Equally, wearing something elegant in a place of worship was important to me. My dress was just as I visualised, with three quarter length sleeves and the blood-red top fitted snugly around my body. My *lengha* had a fishtail design, and my *chunni* flowed from my head bun down my back. My outfit had been made within a month: the designer had done a great job.

There was no turning back now, this was it. Now I just had to ensure that my make-up was meticulously applied to be as flawless as my outfit. It was. When I turned to the mirror, I gasped, scarcely believing the look that had been created. It may have taken hours and cost a fortune, but it was absolutely perfect.

Finally, I could look at myself and see someone beautiful. I could finally say I looked like a bride. In fact, I felt like a celebrity for the first time. The day was perfect, and I believe it was because I was confident my secret would not be revealed. I could enjoy my role as a Bollywood princess and enjoy the experience of being looked at, not just because of my skin.

Six months later, Nev and I waited eagerly to receive our wedding album. It had taken slightly longer to produce, as we had over 2000 photos and a video. Our photographer was very well-known and had a backlog of work to complete, so we were incredibly excited when he came to deliver the album in person.

I was not disappointed; everything was perfect. Of course, I was worried about my skin, but the photos were incredible. I gleamed with relief as I looked to Nev and thanked him for organising such amazing photography and videography.

As I adapted to my married life in West London, my focus then started to shift to my career and my PA role at Gartmore. I loved working there, as the company had a real family feel to it and the people seemed down to earth. I did not have a demanding role and managed to cope with the work quite easily. For the first time, I was in a permanent role, which was a little daunting. There could be no running away like before. I would have to get to know my colleagues and they would get to know me.

But what about my skin? I decided, yet again, to keep it hidden. Fortunately, the office was freezing even in the summer months, so I didn't look too out of place. I felt like I was getting away with my secret again: the air conditioning was the perfect excuse for me to carry on wearing long-sleeved tops without anyone asking any questions. For the first time, I let people get to know me and become close to me. It was a strange feeling, because I had kept my guard up so fervently in other workplaces.

Perhaps the confidence this brought, alongside my experiences tutoring, drove my eventual move towards teaching. However, I still had my concerns, especially about the children. I spoke to Nev.

"Children can be spiteful and malicious. They say things that they do not even realise hurt. What if some child notices my skin and they mock me in the class?

How would I cope?" I was panicking again, hoping Nev could provide the answers there and then.

"If you really want to do this, then maybe now is the time. You may not get an opportunity later," he said. Yet these weren't the only negative thoughts in my mind. Suddenly, I realised I needed to call Sara.

It had been a while since we had spoken. We had lost touch, and I was worried she may not want to speak to me again. The last conversation we had had was about her career. Sara was now teaching. She had followed the path I was now thinking of. I had to get back in touch, not only for this reason, but because I missed her and wanted her back. She was there at my wedding, but things were never quite the same. I had not expressed to her how I was feeling, and I owed it to her to tell her.

"Sara, I'm sorry I pushed you away," I explained. I went on to tell her my reasons for it. It wasn't what I wanted, but it was the way I found it easiest to cope. I told Sara my body was changing by the day and I felt like no one understood. The only way I could get through this was by isolating myself, my thoughts and my personality, because I just could not seem to get through to anyone about what was happening.

"You hurt me, Joti. I tried so hard to reach out, but I just never understood why you didn't take my calls. After everything we went through, living together and sharing a big part of our lives, you totally rejected me. That hurt me a lot."

I was lost for words. I had nothing else I could say to Sara to make her feel better. Sara was clearly hurt, so I decided to leave the teaching conversation for another time. She needed time to digest what I said, and I needed time to think about how to make things right. I decided to give Sara a little space. She said she would call, so I did not want to pester her. I had hurt her enough and wanted to give her time to heal.

One day passed and I did not hear from her. I do not know why this bothered me so much, but a day turned into a week and I started to worry that this was it, I had lost Sara for good. I had hurt her too much and she had given up on our friendship.

Finally, after eight days, the telephone rang. It was Sara, and I was so relieved to hear her voice on the phone.

"Things have been so stressful at school," she explained, telling me how she was becoming increasingly exasperated by the behaviour of the children at the school. This was not what I really wanted to hear, especially as I was thinking about going into teaching myself. We had a lengthy conversation about the pros and cons of teaching, and we never mentioned our period of distance again.

Sara was a friend who I had missed hugely, and she went on to fully support me in applying for a teaching role, asking me some key questions that I had not really asked myself about entering the profession. But, speaking to her, made me even more determined to become a teacher.

My family was supportive and Nev told me that this would be the perfect time to make a career change. I did not have any other commitments, other than him. I loved the way he supported my decisions in everything I did and how he thought I was on the right path.

I started to research my options for university, eventually finding the Institute of Education. I thought the IOE would be the ideal place to continue my postgraduate studies. It was incredibly difficult to get into, but I thought, with my CELTA qualification, degree (Certificate for Language Teaching to Adults) and tutoring experience, I might have a shot. I sat down to write my statement and the words just flowed out. I knew that I was making the right decision: I wanted to share my passion for languages, so this is exactly what I wrote. I then had to sit an interview in person, after which I would be notified by post.

A few weeks later, I received a place at the university. I was delighted to be starting my dream career, using my Spanish to teach children and inspire them to learn.

My life was about to change once again.

Chapter 10 – A Steroid Life

"We cannot change our past.
We cannot change the fact that people act in a certain way.
We cannot change the inevitable.
The only thing we can do is play on the one string
we have, and that is our attitude."
Charles R. Swindoll[10]

By April, most of the people on my course were starting to obtain posts in schools, and it was time for me to start applying too. I am generally quite an organised person, but it wasn't a question of being sloppy: I realised I was afraid of reality. I would be teaching in a secondary school, but what if I could not manage the behaviour there? What if this wasn't the job for me and I was someone they mocked and took advantage of? These thoughts kept niggling at the back of my mind until mid-May arrived, and I saw a post at an outstanding school in Central London. I knew I had to apply quickly, as the teaching positions there were never open for long.

Within a week I had applied for the post. The application involved teaching a Spanish lesson, as well as an interview with the head teacher and the head of languages. Teaching a set of students I had never met before was particularly daunting. This whole job opportunity depended on my lesson and how I delivered it. It made me feel very uptight. What if the students mocked me? What if they noticed my skin and this distracted from how I delivered my lesson?

I had to think positively as I got up that morning for the interview. I had planned what to wear the night before, and all my makeup was neatly placed in the bathroom so I could quickly get ready without added stress the following morning.

I wore a full-length trouser suit and shirt, which would partly cover my hands. This filled me with confidence and ensured my lesson went excellently. I was to teach a mixed-ability Year 8 Spanish group, so I packed the lesson with different learning methods, as there were some higher-achieving girls and some less-gifted ones too. My first experience of classroom teaching was nerve-wracking: I felt like a rabbit entering a dragon's den! Despite my nerves, I successfully secured a position for September and was notified one hour later that I'd got the job by the head of languages.

"Well done Joti, you delivered an outstanding lesson. When we asked the students what they thought, they said they really enjoyed your lesson too. You have a lovely way with them, and that is one of the things we were looking for. Your level of Spanish is amazing too." I had not heard such positive words about me for a while, and I think it was the motivation I needed to regain some confidence.

I was so proud of myself, especially because I had secured a post in a school where behaviour was exceptional, and I knew I would be supported if any issues arose. This was my main concern: if I became a target because of my skin, I wanted to know there were policies in place and the school would deal with the issue accordingly.

At the start of my new teaching career, I felt I would be in this for life. Teaching has always been regarded as a noble career, and I felt some relief that I would have something stable to fall back on throughout my life. Furthermore, I would be using my languages to teach: I had worked so hard to obtain my degree and I was not going to lose the ability and flair developed through my education.

Meanwhile there was still Vitiligo. This was now 60% spread across my body, with the main areas turning white being my arms, legs, chest, back and feet. My hands were now noticeable too. However, I would spend a good hour covering my skin before school. It was easy to apply makeup, and, by this stage, I seemed to have mastered a good cover up technique. This consisted of blending, using multiple brushes to stipple the creamy foundation and blend this in with my patches and brown skin.

Dressing well was important to me, as it had been even before my Vitiligo. My makeup just became a part of that routine, and I became an expert at covering up my Vitiligo and blending makeup in with my outfits. Thus, attention would be paid to what I was wearing rather than my patches. It was a carefully-crafted plan of action that ensured I was not drawing any attention to my skin.

As I became accustomed to a teacher's life, I started to pay a little less attention to my skin. I had other things to focus on; a new job, new students and classes, and new colleagues, too. This created a positive mindset and distracted me from my patches.

At around the same time, I spoke to an osteopath who Gurds had introduced me to through the Vitiligo Society. He'd recently undergone steroid therapy for Vitiligo, and both Gurds and I thought this treatment might be an option for us too. We were keen to find out more. I had never given up hope of finding a treatment and still had dreams of my skin reverting to its normal colour.

After several conversations over a period of months, Gurds and I decided that we would embark on steroid treatment together. It was not openly advertised, but I felt confident from the word-of-mouth review from the osteopath. It had worked for him, and we must have met him about four times before deciding to see the specialist doctor ourselves in Gatwick.

It took a long time for us to get ourselves organised. We wanted to start treatment together, but I had just started my new job and Gurds was working too, so we always found it hard to book a time and get there. At the back of our minds, I think we were afraid: once we started steroids, we knew we would have to commit seriously to it.

After months of waiting, Gurds and I went to visit the doctor at his home. Gurds would be meeting me outside, so I left early to avoid the traffic on the M25. I was pensive: thoughts of positivity and hope mixed with nervousness. Would I be able to cope and manage the intensity of the treatment? It was a long journey, treatment would eat up nearly five hours of my day on the weekends, and I had to work all week. However, knowing I would be undergoing the treatment with Gurds made me feel more secure. At least I would not be alone.

Just five minutes before arrival, I started to feel very nervous. It almost felt like I was on a first date. My stomach started doing somersaults and I was not sure what to expect, but when I saw Gurds waiting in her car, her friendly smile and wave instantly put me at ease.

"Welcome," said the doctor, with a strong Indian accent. He was a short man with short, curly black hair. My first impression was that he did not look like a doctor, and I felt quite wary as he asked us to come inside. However, his wife popped out from inside the lounge and came to greet us too.

"I'm the doctor's wife," she said proudly. Her face, as pale as a white rose, was almost English-looking, but she had an even stronger Indian accent than he did. She asked us if we would like something to drink.

"Just water would be great," I said, as we sat down to wait for the doctor to finish with a patient he was treating. As we sat there, I could tell we both felt the same nerves. After five minutes, the doctor returned, sweaty-faced, and invited us to find out what would be involved in the treatment.

There were tablets, which we needed to take two hours before "light treatment" each day. Then, we would have injections that would start in our hands, feet and legs. Based on their success, we would decide whether to continue or not.

He repeated this information about 3 times until the intensity of the treatment sunk in.

"So, what light do we use?" asked Gurds.

"One like this," said the doctor, pointing to a huge, sunbed-type light that we would each need to purchase and use in addition to the tablets. It was so large that there was no way it would fit in either of our cars, so we decided that we would pick it up at a later date.

This treatment did not come cheap. We paid £200 in cash every two weeks for the tablets and injections. In return, he promised us our pigment back. It was as simple as that. The doctor seemed very confident with his treatment, he had been practicing for 15 years and had many success stories. Apparently, one happy customer was due to arrive just after us.

"You can speak to her. She is 10 years old and has been having treatment with me for a few months. Now, her Vitiligo is nearly all gone."

We felt that the more patients we could speak to, the better, as we wanted to see the evidence ourselves. A few minutes later, the doorbell rang, and the doctor went to answer the door. Gurds and I looked at each other. We were both excited, but still nervous at the prospect having found a solution. This could really be it. Our pigment could come back if we took this seriously and committed ourselves, but we were in disbelief that any treatment could work.

The door opened as the doctor popped his head in to invite us in to meet the girl. She was about the age my daughter is now, 10-years-old, and she smiled at us as we entered. We asked her how she felt doing the treatment, to which her mother responded that her daughter cries every time she has the injections.

I glanced over at Gurds and knew what she was thinking. We were both grown adults who knew what we were letting ourselves in for. On the other hand, did the girl really want to undergo this treatment? Behind her smile, she seemed sad, afraid and scared.

I told her that her skin looked amazing and how great it was that she was responding to treatment. She looked up, but it was not the expression I was hoping to see. I thought she would be over the moon, but she simply wasn't.

Gurds and I did not really speak much after that. The doctor was left to treat her, and we left, knowing that this was going to be intense. The look of that little girl has never left me to this day.

From certainty emerged doubt. Would this be the right path for us? We had initially agreed to chat that very evening, but neither of us called. I was far too exhausted by the time I arrived home, especially because I needed to tell Nev about the first meeting with the doctor. I had no energy to speak, preoccupied by the look in the little girl's sad eyes.

"I'm so confused," I told Nev. I was trying to catch my breath, already exhausted. How would I possibly do this treatment every other week?

"If you really want to do this, you will." Nev was so empathetic, patient and supportive, which is why I married him. He understood me, and he allowed me time to myself to gather my thoughts.

Gurds and I both needed time to figure out if this was going to be the right decision for us both. All I knew was that I missed my brown skin and I wanted to just have it back. It was all I ever dreamt of. Regardless of the pain I would suffer with the injections or the exhausting journey, I decided I would be doing this with or without Gurds.

The next day, she called. "Joti, I'm just not sure about this. I have spoken to my family, and I don't feel that seeing two people with results is enough to convince me."

I felt saddened to be doing this alone, but nothing was holding me back. I had to go through with the treatment as it was my last lifeline and I had to give everything I had.

After just 8 weeks, my first spot of pigment returned. That was a huge turning point for me. Every fresh brown pigment was cause for celebration, it felt like I was on fire, bursting with happiness and pride. I felt hopeful, I felt positive, I felt this was going to be my time at last.

The trickle of pigment became a flow. First were my legs and arms, where some brown spots started to merge, becoming bigger and bigger, eventually joining to form larger brown areas. It was unbelievable, I just could not believe what I was seeing in front of me. Nev was in disbelief. My family were incredibly surprised.

Happiness did not come without pain. Every two weeks, I underwent painful injections and would leave in an emotional wreck. Sometimes I could hardly drive the car, my eyes puffy and blurry with tears.

Even though Gurds was not doing the treatment, we would speak regularly, as she was keen to know how I was doing. Eventually, having seen my results, she started with the treatment too. Our weekends would be planned around going to Gatwick together, and we would give each other encouragement when the other was not feeling as hopeful. Treatment had highs and lows: sometimes it felt like we were making progress, other times we were exhausted from the commute and the treatment itself. It took a lot of energy out of us.

Somehow, I managed to cope working in school too, fitting in my marking in the evenings. The process lasted from October 2007 to January 2010, during which time I had re-pigmented (with some lapses) to about 90% melanin. This was a huge achievement, and I was so thankful to the doctor. The main side effect was weight gain, owing to the steroid injections, but I just accepted this. Seeing my pigment felt more of a priority than my weight or the emotions I had to deal with during this difficult time.

It was incredible. With no information on the internet at the time, Gurds and I had worked so hard to research treatment. Here I was, three years on, with my pigment back.

It felt too good to be true, and... it was. I was about to find out that my brown skin was not going to stay with me for long.

Chapter 11 - I Was a Misfit

"Being different makes me feel so empowered to tell people they don't have to fit in and they can just be themselves."
Joti Gata-Aura

"I think I am pregnant," I said, looking at Nev with disappointment. This was supposed to be one of the happiest days of my life, but I was terribly upset.

"Pregnant?!" There was joy in his eyes, which disappeared when he saw the disappointment in my face and body.

"But what about my treatment? I'm nearly all brown. I've gone through so much pain to get my brown skin back... so why now?" It sounds terrible, but this is how I felt. This is what I was going through, what Vitiligo had done to my body. It took a lot from me, and getting my brown pigment back was important. Being pregnant meant that I could not finish the last 10% of treatment, my chance to be normal like everyone else.

What about my hard work? What about my body and how I feel? What about my emotions? This is my skin, this is my body. Surely I have the right to choose.

Of course, I was happy I was having a baby, happy to be pregnant. Yet I needed to express what Vitiligo had done to me. This was the first time I'd had control of my body for years, the first time I'd seen results, so I was bound to be conflicted. I wanted to finish the treatment, but as days passed by, I knew I would not be able to.

It was a hard reality to face. A tiny bit of me was relieved, because it also meant I was free of the burden the treatment brought. I was becoming exhausted from the travel to and from the doctor, and I was enduring such pain across all areas of my body on a bi-weekly basis. Sometimes this pain would linger on for days.

Gurds and I would always try to attend appointments together, and she held my hand like a mother as I was pricked and prodded all over. I was there for her too. We would clench our hands to transfer positive energy to each other, which kept us going for the next couple of years. Nev always supported me too. He could feel and see the intensity of the treatment, so he understood the distress and agony I was in. It made me realise how lucky I was to have him.

However, my time was up with the treatment. I would no longer be able to keep going now that I had a baby to care for. I felt like I would be letting Gurds down, but I knew I had to put myself first. It was the best decision I could have made, because having put so much into the treatment, I had no more energy to give. Whatever I had would have to go to my baby. I finally let Gurds and the doctor know about my decision, then stopped treatment immediately.

I had waited for so long for a miracle, to see my skin brown, and I was looking forward to being myself again: no more worrying about camouflage makeup and short sleeves. However, I now had a baby to look after, so priorities shifted to her. As weeks passed, my steroid treatment was becoming a distant memory. My body would start to go through further changes as I carried this precious soul inside of me. In October 2010, she came into the world.

Later I found out that Gurds had given up treatment too. After a trip to Dubai, she noticed some white patches reappear and lost hope of the treatment providing results. I too had new patches. We both felt such regret that we had invested so much time, effort and money into this treatment, only for it to reverse.

However, I was now busy with my daughter. The night feeds and irregular routine of looking after her kept my mind occupied. I was a keen mother, wanting to make fresh food for my baby, learn about the new products on the market and be the best I could for my little girl.

Before she was born, I had attended antenatal classes, where I met a lovely girl who proved to be very supportive during the first few years of motherhood. Nisha was someone who I instantly bonded with. A confident, bubbly, and pretty girl, our friendship developed through our pregnancies and having our baby daughters together. My Vitiligo was not obvious at the time, following the success of the steroid treatment, so I was not overly worried about meeting her socially.

The first months of my pregnancy flew by: I had never felt better about myself, I had brown skin and I was looking after my baby by exercising regularly. It started to feel like I was rebuilding my life and learning to love myself from the beginning again. It was an incredible experience to be doing this with my baby too. This was a fresh start, and I wanted to embrace all these new changes that lay ahead of me.

I realised I wanted to share my skin journey with Nisha. We met up for coffee and shared a good baby chat. Most of our get-togethers would revolve around baby talk: baby food, baby routine and tips on what was working and not working.

It helped to have someone who was going through the same as I was, even a little ahead of me in the game. She would always share her strategies with me, which made things a little easier. I was blessed to have her around. I had kept many people at arm's length before, but Nisha was different: I believe she came into my life for a reason.

We became close very quickly, and when she was expecting her second child, a boy, I followed suit. My own son was to be born four months after hers. We developed a solid friendship and, even though she is seven years younger than me, I am in awe of her resilience, strength, determination and morals. She is a loyal and genuine friend, who is always there for me and so many others. Even today with four children, she will always pick up the phone and ask how I am.

While I was pregnant with my son, my Vitiligo was reverting: white patches were appearing again. This did worry me, not least because at some point, I would have to talk to Nisha about my Vitiligo. I did not mention my skin to her for two years, but one day we decided to meet up at her place. As we were both breastfeeding, I knew she would notice anyway.

"Nish," I started anxiously, worried about her reaction. "Have you noticed these white spots on my skin?"

"I have. There is nothing wrong with it, it makes you individual and unique, and I think it looks cool! Here, look at my tattoo," she finished. I do not think she meant to change the topic of conversation, but that is when I started to realise that, maybe, Vitiligo wasn't the end of the world. It was certainly a refreshing experience, and one of the first encounters I had with someone who really was not bothered about what I looked like. Instantly, something changed inside of me. I felt lighter because she did not judge me.

Towards the end of my maternity leave in 2012, I made another decision. I started at a new school, closer to home, which turned out to be hugely beneficial. My previous school could not offer me part-time work, and while I wanted to carry on teaching, I had to be closer to home. I needed to work part-time to balance work with raising a family. I knew I could not let go of work, but I also wanted to be there for my young children at Christmas concerts, parents' evenings and the like. To be fully present in their lives, I searched for part-time positions that would give me the best of both worlds.

Gumley was my safety net. I had joined a school with values that boosted my confidence even more.

Excellence, Gentleness, Justice, Companionship, Hope and Dignity were the key tenets of the institution, but I did not realise until later how much these would help me.

Four years later, I was fully settled into what felt like a big family environment. The staff cared for each other and the students were kind, polite and different to any I had ever taught before. I found myself in a magical environment: I loved teaching and most of all the respect and the values we shared together. I felt part of a community, accepted by my colleagues and students alike. I had never experienced this at my former school or in banking, so it was the first time I truly felt valued and respected for my skills, not my looks.

Despite this, at my new school I continued to wear long-sleeved tops, as the patches had returned a couple of years after joining. If anything, my Vitiligo was now spreading faster than before.

I reverted to panic, covering up and applying my makeup before work in a one-hour routine. I had almost forgotten what this looked like, as I had become accustomed to not having to apply any makeup in the intermittent time. I started to find things difficult. I had to get up early before school started, ensuring that all my spots were covered. Working in the city was one thing, but now, with 30 sets of eyes on me, I had to ensure that nothing was on show at all. Ultimately, I longed to be free in the skin I was in. I wanted to be free of makeup, but I worried what my colleagues and students would say.

I felt like I wanted to do something bigger for myself. I needed to get back in touch with the Vitiligo Society. I hadn't been in contact since 2007, when I saw that my pigment was returning: I simply hadn't needed them then. However, here I was knocking on the Society's door again.

When I called them, a lovely lady called Natalie picked up the phone. I explained my situation to her. I had been part of the society in 1999, but hadn't renewed my newsletters because I thought steroid treatment would work. She took time to listen to me, engaged in conversation, and we talked about my Vitiligo journey.

Then, as we were about to end the call she said, "Joti, I was just wondering. We have been approached by the BBC and I wanted to ask if you'd be interested in taking part in a TV documentary?"

I was taken aback. My natural answer would, of course, be no, but as Natalie talked more, I started to feel more positive. What would it mean if I were to take part in it? I told Natalie I would have a think about it, then agreed to take part a few days later.

I spoke to the producer, who not only interviewed me in person, but on the phone a couple of times too. He confirmed that I would be perfect for the show.

"It would be great to have an older figure on a show who has children," he said. I wasn't sure how much younger the others were, but I relished the idea of taking this step. I felt ready and knew it was the right call.

Misfits Like Us aired on the BBC1 on June 12, 2016. It was an empowering journey of self-love, self-discovery, and self-empowerment: another huge turning point for me, to appear with sleeveless clothing. I had never done this before in any social situation, let alone on national TV, and it was a huge step towards embracing my skin.

When the documentary was aired, I was extremely nervous. I knew that some of my story would be out there and now there would be no turning back. Equally, this was a pivotal moment that allowed me to let go of the person I was and step into the shoes of a stronger one.

Shortly after the show was aired, with support from my school, I took part in some motivational assemblies and talks to a range of year groups. The school really embraced the topic of body positivity, and as I led these talks, I realised that I too wanted to be freer in the skin I was in. I was still wearing makeup to work at the time, but, a year later in 2017, I entered school without any makeup on.

I then started to confide in another Spanish teacher, who I had become close to. I told her all about my skin condition and that I wanted to start being more open about my skin. As we sat in our office together, I looked at her.

"Should I take my cardigan off?" I asked.

"Do it!" she said. Maria was a supportive colleague and friend, and I felt I could trust her. It was another milestone at a point when I was getting fed up with hiding my skin. It was a pleasant spring morning and I felt warmer than usual. Without any further hesitation, I whipped my cardigan off. I was expecting some curiosity from members of staff and the students, but there was no reaction. No look, no stare, just nothing.

How bizarre. Just what exactly are people thinking? Are they not bothered about looking at my white skin? Why am I so bothered? Why am I worrying about the students pointing and making fun of me?

I was becoming mentally stronger without even realising it. The atmosphere at school was empowering me: during assemblies, I heard colleagues speaking to students, offering wisdom and strength, and it had an effect on me too. I would deliver prayers and quotes to my tutor group, which supported my own mindset and confidence too. I absorbed the reflections, assemblies, prayers, poetry and speeches made by staff, which inspired me to change my life and how I saw things around me.

Students came to me for support with a range of body issues. This was an extremely rewarding feeling: not only was I their Spanish teacher, I was their role model too. Some of my students say I am like their mother at school, as they feel comfortable discussing a variety of issues with me. This only makes me feel more fulfilled, knowing I am supporting so many students as they mature into the world.

Sometimes I would get emails or a quick comment from students, telling me how I supported them and gave them the confidence to accept who they are. I wanted to do more. I wanted to support others and help them on their journeys, so I decided to set up a small social media page to document my journey so far. At first, I just replied to the messages of support: many said that I was brave to go on TV and talk about my Vitiligo. Then, I tried to support those who had been diagnosed and did not know where to turn.

I knew I had to be there for the people who were suffering like I had, to offer them hope and guidance. Some evenings, my inbox overflowed with messages, and I would sift through some disturbing comments about how people were feeling.

I wouldn't let anyone feel alone. I knew what isolation was. I experienced loneliness with Vitiligo and it was a dark place to be.

I believe I was placed on earth to help and support others, and this will be my mission forever. For years, it was all about receiving, and now I was able to give back and offer something to others. It was a unique and special feeling to be able to do this, both at school and on social media. Giving back to society and helping people is only something you feel from your heart, but you want to do more when you know the impact it has on people's lives.

From just one documentary, my life changed forever. As someone who once hid her skin, changing the perceptions of others is an incredible feeling.

It has grown into such a positive aspect of my life now. My goal is central to my beliefs, feelings, empathy and love towards other people with visible skin conditions and other disabilities. It has launched into something I never knew I would be able to create.

Chapter 12 - Being Positively Diverse

"Be Seen, Be Heard, Be You!"
Joti Gata-Aura @PositivelyDiverse

I launched @vitiligo_and_me in April 2018. It was an account for me to start writing and sharing my journey with people struggling with their body image. I wanted to keep it private at first, as I still had not accepted my skin completely, and there were still a lot of people who did not know about my condition. I had never written about Vitiligo, but found the approach very therapeutic and a great way to gain control of my emotions.

As I started to describe my life living with Vitiligo, I did not know that my account would resonate with so many people. It felt strange to share my story with others, particularly because I kept my skin hidden for so long, but it was also hugely empowering. I started to receive multiple messages daily, from people all over the world asking for help and support.

In these messages, people told me how they had just been diagnosed, while others asked about which treatments I had used. Many just wanted to be heard, but others were in a very dark place close to suicide.

Vitiligo is often overlooked, or not taken seriously, because it is not considered life threatening. However, in doing so, people fail to realise the mental and emotional battle that must be overcome. These white patches cause many of us to feel ashamed and embarrassed, or cause us to fall into isolation.

I was touched, but equally surprised, at how many people were affected by the condition around the world. Social media brought us all together. It was a place to seek sanctuary and support. There was a real Vitiligo community growing, which was something that would have seemed absurd to me years ago.

I needed to share my experience of living with Vitiligo: how I coped during and after pregnancy and working in the city. I had to overcome so many little hurdles in my life, so I knew I was able to help people who were finding the whole process difficult.

I had already taken some steps forward, including my documentary. As I was now a little ahead in my self-acceptance, I knew I was able to support the many people who were just beginning. I felt this was my time to start giving back. As I started to support people, I realised just how much self-doubt had affected me during the initial years, leaving me feeling hopeless and unable to control my body. I was now in a strong position mentally and I was ready to give everything I had.

I started to invest more and more time into supporting other people with their Vitiligo, especially regarding their emotional and mental health. I was also approached by several media outlets to share my story. I went onto various BBC radio shows, including the BBC Asian Network. I wrote for magazines to discuss the importance of self-worth and self-acceptance regarding Vitiligo.

I started to wear less makeup as I did this, highlighting the importance of representation, inclusivity, and diversity. I never thought that I would ever take part in London Fashion Week, but this is exactly what happened in 2020: a life-changing moment for me.

Through these empowering projects, I met some wonderful people who, like myself, had gone through life-changing experiences. I was keen to hear about their stories and find out how we could work together to make the world a better place, especially through education.

I decided I wanted to start interviewing people and build on thought-provoking discussions, raising awareness and building a better understanding of people's differences and disabilities. This is when I rebranded myself as Positively Diverse. Now, through my YouTube and social media platforms, I focus not just on highlighting Vitiligo, but discussing a variety of skin conditions and disabilities. This emphasizes the importance of difference to the media.

I love listening to other people's stories. We all have our challenges, differences and difficulties with our bodies.

Young people are under tremendous pressure nowadays, especially with regard to their looks. Social media is central to this, which is worrying: it can influence young people's education negatively, causing them to become distracted from their learning. According to the Mental Health Foundation[11], a survey of young people aged 11-16 by Be Real found that 79% said that how they look is important to them. Over half (52%) often worry about how they look. Of young people aged 13-19, body image was "often" or "always" a worry for 35% of them. Those in the 16-25 age bracket identify their appearance as their third biggest challenge.

I love the community online and the people I have met on my social media platforms. Some have a compelling story to tell, many have gone through life-changing experiences, and all have something positive to share with the world. I believe I cannot spread my message of body positivity alone, and the most important thing is that we are all in this experience together.

I have collaborated extensively with different brands, designers and media outlets to spread my message of body positivity. We need more diversity, inclusivity and representation in the media. However, this relies on people who want to be seen and heard. I try to lend them a voice to highlight their challenges in the world we are living in today.

As a mother of a ten-year-old daughter and an eight-year-old son, also having worked in teaching for 17 years, I feel so passionate about the topic of body positivity. I want my children to grow up with self-love from a young age. I want them to know themselves and feel confident with loving themselves just the way they are. My experience with the students I teach tells me the world is a scary place: it is intimidating, and if you are not strong enough you can fall victim to bullying, online and in social environments.

I feel our children need to be equipped with the right tools from a young age, which is why I now speak about a range of visible and hidden disabilities on my platform. I'm challenging stereotypes and bringing more media attention to disabilities and skin conditions that need to be understood.

I believe no one should feel isolated or suffer alone. There is a wealth of support online, so please reach out and talk to someone: that one person could change your life. With the right mindset, you'll soon be in a better place, just like I am.

Vitiligo came into my world as an uninvited guest and turned my whole life upside down. It traumatized me, left me completely bereft and often searching for a reason to go on.

But now, with hindsight, I see that I am on the path that I need to be on. Without Vitiligo I would not have met so many people who came into my life and had such an impact on it. Without Vitiligo I would not be connecting with others with the same condition. Without Vitiligo I would not have had some of the opportunities I have had. Without Vitiligo I would not be the strong person I am today.

No – I am not glamorizing this condition. I am, however, saying that I have come to accept my Vitiligo. For the first time in my life, I can happily and confidently say "I am *Strong In The Skin I'm In*".

Further Information

The charities and organizations I have listed below are the ones I have recommended or have used personally. The books below are the ones that have supported me in my skin journey.

The Vitiligo Society- if you or anyone else has been affected by Vitiligo, you can contact the society directly below.
https://vitiligosociety.org/

The British Skin Foundation- This is an excellent organization that supports with all visual skin conditions.
https://www.britishskinfoundation.org.uk/

The British Association of Dermatologists
https://www.bad.org.uk/

Further Reading

The Mojatu Foundation
https://www.mojatufoundation.org/mental-health-in-the-british-asian-community/
accessed May 2021

Mind Charity
https://www.mind.org.uk/information-support/types-of-mental-health-problems/mental-health-problems-introduction/about-mental-health-problems/
accessed May 2021

NHS
https://www.nhs.uk/conditions/vitiligo/
accessed May 2021

Quote Credits

Every effort has been made to correctly credit the quote sources, but if any have been inadvertently overlooked or incorrectly referenced, please contact the publishers or the author.

Chapter 1
[1]Eminem. Eminem Quotes. Brainy Quote.com,
https://www.brainyquote.com/quotes/eminem_387440
accessed May 2021

Chapter 2
[2]Laura Ingalls Wilder. Laura Ingalls Wilder Quotes. Brainy Quote.com,
https://www.brainyquote.com/quotes/laura_ingalls_wilder_1264
25
accessed June 2021

Chapter 3
[3]Morihei Ueshiba. Morihei Ueshiba Quotes. Brainy Quote.com,
https://www.brainyquote.com/quotes/morihei_ueshiba_183597
accessed May 2021

Chapter 4
[4] Mary J. Blige. Mary J. Blige Quotes. Brainy Quote.com,
https://www.brainyquote.com/quotes/mary_j_blige_593875
accessed February 2021

Chapter 5
[5] Bill Watterson. Bill Watterson Quotes. Brainy Quote.com,
https://www.brainyquote.com/quotes/bill_watterson_383142
accessed May 2021

Chapter 6
[6] John McCain. John McCain Quotes. Brainy Quote.com,
https://www.brainyquote.com/quotes/john_mccain_135484
accessed May 2021

[7] The Mojatu Foundation,
 https://www.mojatufoundation.org/#
accessed February 2021

Chapter 7
[8] Lou Holtz. Lou Holtz Quotes. Brainy Quote.com,
https://www.brainyquote.com/quotes/lou_holtz_450789
accessed June 2021

Chapter 8
[9] Harvey Fierstein, Harvey Fierstein Quotes, Brainy Quote.com,
https://www.brainyquote.com/quotes/harvey_fierstein_461688
accessed March 2021

Chapter 10
[10] Charles R.Swindoll. Charles R.Swindoll Quotes, Brainy
Quote.com,
https://www.brainyquote.com/quotes/charles_r_swindoll_16338
5
accessed April 2021

[11] The Mental Health Foundation
https://www.mentalhealth.org.uk/publications/body-image-
report/childhood
accessed June 2021

Photo and Design Credits

Cover Design by Angela Basker

Front Cover:
Positively Diverse Branding – Rachel Kepinska-Smith
Cover Photograph – Alison J Burrows

Back Cover:
Author Photograph – Lightning Media
Illustration – Ineta Švedaitè

Acknowledgements

To my children Ria and Dilan, who continue to support me and have always encouraged me to write and share my Vitiligo story. I know this book will be with you for life, I love you so much and hope you remember to always be you in this world that lies ahead of you. I am so proud of you and everything you have achieved so far and hope you feel inspired by everything mummy has achieved.

To my husband Nev, thank you for being there for me from day one when I was the brown girl to changing into a white girl. Thank you for your continued support and love in all that I do. You have always been my rock and shown that our love is so much more than skin deep which makes me realise our marriage is truly very special and unique.

To my wonderful family. Dad, I lost you a few years ago, but I know you are looking down on me and I know you are giving me the strength to do this because this is what you built in me, resilience and courage. I miss you hugely and know you would be surprised, and proud, at how far I have come in my skin journey.

Mum, you are the strength that holds our family together. You have done so much to support others and I admire how tough you are which has given me such empowerment and determination in my skin journey.

Thank you to my in-laws for never judging me and taking me in wholeheartedly and accepting me for my changing skin throughout the years and always having my back.

Shilpa you are the backbone of the Positively Diverse YouTube channel and your support with other social media has been invaluable.

Rachel, you brought my brand Positively Diverse alive in such a coherent and powerful way. Thank you for encouraging and believing in me.

Shani your foreword will resonate with so many people on disability inclusion and is a great way to start my book. I am very grateful for your contribution.

Shalini, you gave me the opportunity to be part of an incredible process of sharing my story openly. Through your Pen to Published course, (together with Ami and Rosie my fellow writers), you have supported me throughout my writing journey. Your vast experience and wealth of knowledge on writing and publishing has given me the ability to confidently put together this memoir.

The colleagues at my school, especially the deputy head, Fiona Russell, thank you for supporting me and encouraging me to lead on the motivational assemblies to the students at our school.

To all my lovely friends including Shalini, Nisha, Gurds, Maria, Lidia, Natalie and Manisha. You all supported me and kept me afloat. Your words of wisdom have given me the confidence to come out and be myself. Thank you for everything.

Finally, thank you Sara for being such a supportive friend to me since university and until today and letting me share our experiences of what we went through in my book. You are a loyal friend and I am truly grateful for your support and love.

About The Author

Joti Gata-Aura is a British Sikh brought up in London. She pursued her passion for languages working as a teacher for 16 years. She married with two children and runs a business called Positively Diverse; championing better representation in the media for those with visible differences and disabilities. She works in the media in presenting on body positivity to spread and raise awareness of Vitiligo and other skin conditions and disabilities by breaking down barriers in society and within the Asian Community.

Pen to Published

*A 6-month programme that will enable you to
write, publish and promote your book*
with Amazon bestselling author <u>Shalini Bhalla-Lucas</u>

You know you have a book in you.
You just don't know how to get it out there...
Let me show you how.

With my Zoom programme you will be able to get your ideas
down on paper and be published online on Amazon in SIX
months. The programme will keep you focused and accountable
– which is what you need when you want to
successfully write, publish and promote your book.

*I have been trying to write this book for years, but every time I sat
down in front of the laptop the task seemed enormous and out of reach.
Through "Pen to Published", Shalini provided us with the skills and
techniques to break the process down. Under her expert guidance, and
with the support of the rest of the first-time authors, writing my book
not only became achievable but also one of the most enjoyable
experiences of my life.* **Rosie Miles, Malawi**

*I have started writing a book many times, but lacked the time and
motivation to get past a couple of chapters. "Pen to Published" gave me
the structure and accountability I needed, plus incredible support from
Shalini and her knowledge around writing, formatting, editing and
publishing. I set out with the aim to come out of lockdown as an author
and I achieved it!* **Ami Lauren, Devon**

For more information about Pen to Published please email
<u>info@justjhoom.co.uk</u> **or visit www.justjhoom.co.uk**

Printed in Great Britain
by Amazon

38368066R00098